Table of Contents

Abundant Christianity 1

PART ONE: BECOMING ABUNDANT IN PERSONAL PRAYER 2

1.1 PRAYING ... THE WORD (DAVID WOODS) 3

1.2 PRAYING ... IN THE SPIRIT (KARL SMITH) 8

1.3 PRAYING ... IN THE NAME (GERALDE MAG-USARA) 12

1.4 PRAYING ... IN FAITH AND RIGHTEOUSNESS (ANDY SEDDON) 17

PART 2 – ABUNDANT BIBLE STUDY 21

2.1 STUDYING WITH YOUR HEART (KARL SMITH) 22

2.2 FINDING A BIBLE VERSION AND USING IT (KARL SMITH) .. 27

2.3 4 KEYS TO UNDERSTANDING YOUR BIBLE (BRIAN JOHNSTON) 32

2.4 AN INTRODUCTION TO SYSTEMATIC BIBLE STUDY (MARTIN ARCHIBALD) 37

PART 3 – ABUNDANT CHURCH LIFE 46

3.1 COLLECTIVE LEARNING THAT LIVES (JAMES NEEDHAM) . 47

3.2 COLLECTIVE FELLOWSHIP THAT FUNCTIONS (STEVE SEDDON) 51

3.3 COLLECTIVE WORSHIP THAT WARMS (CRAIG JONES) 57

3.4 COLLECTIVE PRAYER THAT POWERS (BRIAN JOHNSTON) 61

PART 4: ABUNDANT WORSHIP 66

4.1 WHAT IS WORSHIP? (STEPHEN MCCABE) 67

4.2 WORSHIPPING GOD (JAMES NEEDHAM) 72

4.3 INDIVIDUAL WORSHIP AND SACRIFICE (DAVE WEBSTER) . 76

4.4 THE COLLECTIVE WORSHIP OF THE PEOPLE OF GOD (RICHARD HUTCHINSON) 80

PART 5: ABUNDANT GIVING 84

5.1 GIVING TO GOD (EDWIN NEELY) 85

5.2 GIVING TO SUPPORT OTHERS (GARETH ANDREWS) 90

5.3 GIVING TO BUILD GOD'S HOUSE (ANDY SEDDON) 94

5.4 CHEERFUL GIVING (LENNIE SHAW) 98

PART 6: ABUNDANT MARRIAGES 102

6.1 MAKING A MARRIAGE WORK – COMMUNICATION (GEOFF HYDON) 103

6.2 MAKING A MARRIAGE WORK – UNCONDITIONAL LOVE AND RESPECT (KEITH DORRICOTT) 106

6.3 MAKING A MARRIAGE WORK – ENCOURAGEMENT AND FORGIVENESS (DAVE WEBSTER) 108

6.4 MAKING A MARRIAGE WORK – UNSELFISHNESS AND LOYALTY (GREG NEELY) 110

PART 7 – ABUNDANT PERSONAL EVANGELISM 112

7.1 OVERCOMING DEFENCES TO THE GOSPEL (BRIAN JOHNSTON) 113

7.2 CROSSING THE EMOTIONAL MOAT (TONY JONES) 116

7.3 SCALING THE INTELLECTUAL WALL (KARL SMITH) 121

7.4 STORMING THE TOWER OF THE WILL (DAVE WEBSTER) .. 126

ABUNDANT CHRISTIANITY: SEVEN WAYS TO BECOME MORE FRUITFUL AND EFFECTIVE IN FOLLOWING JESUS

© Copyright Hayes Press 2019

PUBLISHED BY:

HAYES PRESS Publisher, Resources & Media,

The Barn, Flaxlands

Royal Wootton Bassett

Swindon, SN4 8DY

United Kingdom

www.hayespress.org

Scripture quotations marked RV are from the Revised Version Bible (1885, Public Domain). Scriptures marked NKJV are from the HOLY BIBLE, the New King James Version® (NKJV®). Copyright © 1982 Thomas Nelson, Inc. Used by permission. All rights reserved. Scriptures marked NIV are from New International Version®, NIV® Copyright © 1973, 1978, 1984, 2011 by Biblica, Inc.™ Used by permission. All rights reserved worldwide. Scriptures marked NASB are from the New American Standard Bible®, Copyright © 1960, 1962, 1963, 1968, 1971, 1972, 1973, 1975, 1977, 1995 by The Lockman Foundation. Used by permission (www.Lockman.org). Scripture quotations marked ESV are from The ESV® Bible (The Holy Bible, English Standard Version®), copyright © 2001 by Crossway, a publishing ministry of Good News Publishers. Used by permission. All rights reserved.

PART ONE: BECOMING ABUNDANT IN PERSONAL PRAYER

Most Christians know that prayer is a vital ingredient for the disciple to grow closer to God and draw from God's unlimited resources of grace and power; and yet there seem to be relatively few Christians who would testify that they regularly experience fruitful times of prayer – in fact many Christians feel that their prayer times are dry and barren and they are left wondering if there prayers went any higher than the ceiling.

In this section of the book are four short chapters designed to help. Firstly, David Woods explores the approach of using God's word as a direct basis for prayer and meditation, recognizing that the very words of Scripture are very powerful and very meaningful. Then Karl Smith looks at the important topic of praying in the Spirit, something that can transform our prayer experience.

Although we can often end our prayers by saying "in Jesus' name, Amen", perhaps we don't fully appreciate what these words actually mean – and as Geralde Mag-usara explains, these words are vitally important and mean a lot!

And finally, Andy Seddon looks at some of the prerequisites that must be in place before we can expect to have an abundant prayer life – the presence of faith and righteousness, as opposed to unbelief and sin, in our lives.

1.1 PRAYING ... THE WORD (DAVID WOODS)

I need to pray scripture. Why? Because my self-generated expressions of prayer are so often narcissistic, irreverent, misguided and faithless. If I am to live (1) and pray, that God may be glorified my prayers cannot just be about me and what I think is best for life; they must be about God, and what He says is best for this life. God's Word is the source and basis of our new life in Christ (2). God's Word also sustains and shapes our faith, repeatedly showing us God's holy character and His perfect outworking of His eternal purposes in this world (3). That's why a craving for God's Word, satisfied by regular consumption through reading and meditation, is an indicator of true and genuine faith in God (4). And to employ God's Word in prayer makes perfect sense!

While revealing the glory of God and His eternal purposes of grace, scripture at the same time reveals the wickedness of my intrinsic sinfulness when unsaved (5). Yes, by God's grace, through faith, I have been born again and my sins are forgiven, but the old nature remains and taints everything about me; sin pervades almost every thought and action (6). I must be careful that what I say is not motivated by sinful and selfish desires because God will not hear (7).

How, then, can I guard against praying selfish prayers that are all about me and my puny perspective of life's circumstances? The solution seems quite simple! I must:

(1) speak back to God what He has revealed about Himself and humanity,

(2) recount how God has dealt with His people in the past, and

(3) remind him of His repeated promises to His people.

All of this is found in God's Word. So, I pray using scripture! That is to say, carefully applying statements found in the Bible to what I say, not just thoughtlessly repeating well-worn texts.

I don't know of many Christians who say that prayer comes easily, or naturally. Is the prayer-struggle that so many of us experience due to the fact that we've, for too long, been praying according to our own ideas and methods? Have we been ignoring the power of employing God's Word as we speak with Him? I've discovered that when incorporating God's Word into my prayer life, God has taken me into a deeper relationship with Him. I'm learning that my relationship with God, and my growing understanding of His ways, is not dependent on my fluctuating affections, inconsistent intellect and commitment levels, but is instead founded on His unchangeable nature and eternal promises. This is transformative (8)!

For many people Bible-time seems to be easier than prayer-time. If that's so, can I suggest something basic? Weave your prayer time into your focus-time in God's Word. The two, of necessity, go hand in hand! As God speaks to us through His Word, we grapple with how it affects our lives and the situations we're concerned about. This is really the starting point of praying God's Word - seeing how what God reveals of Himself and His ways impacts the very circumstances of life we're facing right now. This simple method not only sustains prayer; it results in a greater understanding of God's Word. Of course, it means that we must give sufficient time to our reading-prayer exercise - and that requires planning. If we miss the planning, we'll miss the prayer.

Grappling with God's Word, and speaking God's Word back to Him, is following in the footsteps of the great pray-ers of the Bible. Take Daniel. His prayer, Daniel 9:1-19, flows from his reading of Jeremiah where the Lord spoke about the 70-years' extent of Judah's captivity in Babylon (9). Daniel, a captive in Babylon, prays to understand how God's promises are going to be worked out, particularly since the prophesied 70-year period is almost complete! He's excited to pray about something so soon to be realised!

Notice, also, how Daniel's prayer is full of his knowledge of the Law of Moses and the account of God's dealings with Israel since their exodus. Daniel's prayer is essentially an appeal to God that's based on what God has said about Himself, what God has said He will do for His people, and what God has already done for His people. It's praying scripture!

Take Moses: when interceding on behalf of sinful Israel (10), Moses appeals to God to be faithful to His own revelation of Himself, and to His promises. Moses had encountered God through the burning bush (11), learning about God's great name (12) and His purposes for Israel (13). That experience fuels Moses' prayer, and he also draws on what he knows about God's promises to Abraham, Isaac and Jacob. His prayer is again essentially an appeal to God that's based on what God has revealed about Himself, what God has said He will do for His people, and what God has promised to do for His people. It's praying scripture!

Take the believers in Acts 4:23-31: in the face of growing persecution, the believers gather for a prayer session that literally shakes the building. Look at how, and what, they prayed. They speak to God about who He is, and then recount the words of David from Psalm 2. They see how Psalm 2 applies to their recent history and their present experience, and they appeal to God to continue to work out His purposes according to His glorious will, despite the risk to themselves. The believers' prayer is once again essentially an appeal to God that's based on what God has revealed about Himself, what God has already done for His people, and what God has promised He will do for His people. It's praying scripture.

The actual prayers of the Bible are a rich resource for us to tap into when we're struggling to know how and what to pray. In a sense, they make it easier for us to know what we should be saying to God! If we employ the themes and words of the Bible's prayers, we'll be guarded from the *empty phrases* the Lord criticised the Gentiles for in Matthew 6:7. To avoid such emptiness the Lord gave a model **form** of prayer that's so helpful - see Matthew 6:9-13. It begins with a statement of our understanding of who God is, and what He is doing, which results in worship. It continues with our desire to know and see God's kingdom purposes, followed by a stated commitment to be part of God's work in this world. It then moves into requests for the necessities of daily life, but quickly steps to requests that have to do with good relationships with God and with others. And there's the closing appeal to be kept from temptation and delivered from evil. The 'Lord's Prayer' is a memorable guide when we're struggling with how to pray.

But when it comes to the **substance** of prayer the Apostle Paul's prayers are particularly instructive. In his letters, the early gospel pioneer shares what and who he prays for, how he prays, when he prays, and why he prays. Even a brief study of his prayers will soon expose our own lack of 'prayer etiquette,' and reveal that our often-repeated prayer focus points is not the stuff of Paul's prayers! Many church prayer gatherings can be consumed with prayers for those who are struggling with illness, those who are active in 'frontline' evangelism, and with local church outreach activities. We don't see that same prayer burden in Paul's life; not to the same degree, anyway.

Paul's focus is more:

- the spiritual maturation of disciples, that they might know more deeply the riches of the grace and glory of God, and be consumed by God's sovereign greatness and desire to partner with Him in His kingdom purposes in the world and thereby bear fruit for God's glory (14).

- that there would be unity of purpose and practice, and that individual gospel transformation will result in harmonious and effective church testimony, and that the believers would know joy and strength in their believing (15).

- that doors will be opened to facilitate the spread of the word of God, and that the sharing of the gospel will be effective, and that the resolve of believers to work for God will be realised (16).

Be honest with yourself before God - are your personal prayer burdens similar to Paul's? Is the prayer gathering of your local church characterised by such prayer focus? Pray using scripture. It's the word of truth (17). It will shape our prayers and transform our lives as we speak it back to God. And be encouraged to persist, because *The prayer of a righteous person has great power as it is working* (17).

References: (1) 1 Cor.10:31 (2) 1 Pet.1:23; Rom.10:17; Jas.1:18; Acts 7:38; Rom.3:2 (3) 1 Thess.2:13 (4) 1 Pet.2:2; Heb.5:12-13 (5) Rom.3:10-12 (6) Rom.7:15-20 (7) Ps.66:18 (8) 2 Cor.3:18 (9) Jer.25:1-14 (10) see Ex.32:11-14 (11) see Ex.3 (12) Ex.3:13-14 (13) Ex.3:7-10 (14) e.g. Eph.1:15-22; Eph.3:14-21; Col.1:3-14 (15) e.g. 1 Cor.1:4; Phil.1:9; Col.1:3-14; 1 Thess.3:11-13 (16) e.g. Rom.15:30-33; Eph.6:19-20; Col.4:2-4; 2 Thess.1:11 (17) 2 Tim.2:15 (18) Jas.5:16b

Bible quotations from the ESV.

1.2 PRAYING ... IN THE SPIRIT (KARL SMITH)

Prayer in the Spirit is something we are told to do *at all times*.(1) This makes it one of the defining activities of life, like eating. Before explaining what it involves, however, let's contrast it with a similar expression from another of Paul's letters. In the apostle Paul's time, the mystical experience of speaking in tongues seems often to have been used not only as a testifying sign accompanying the gospel, as in Acts 2, but also in prayer. It seemingly provided an outlet for people to commune with God beyond the confines of mere words in their native language. It must have given those who enjoyed such moments a great sense of liberty. Using this gift in public prayers, however, was discouraged: *For if I pray in a tongue, my spirit prays but my mind is unfruitful. What am I to do? I will pray with my spirit, but I will pray with my mind also (2).*

This praying **with** the spirit seems to me different from praying in the Spirit. In the first of these phrases we may well surmise that Paul has in mind our human spirits *(with my spirit)*, whereas Eph.6:18 and Jude 1:20 clearly have in mind praying **in the Holy Spirit.** Nevertheless, it shows that prayer is a spiritual activity and not just a mental activity. Mind and spirit should be engaged together.

Another interesting difference between these terms is that prayer in the Spirit is meant to be an experience open to every believer. Not all believers spoke in tongues in New Testament times3 and they certainly did not do so constantly. By contrast, Paul encouraged the Ephesian Christians to be found *praying at all times in the Spirit, with all prayer and supplication* (1). The other passage that uses this phrase is Jude 1:20-21: *But you, beloved, building yourselves up in your most holy faith and praying in the Holy Spirit, keep yourselves in the love of God, waiting for the mercy of our Lord Jesus Christ that leads to eternal life.* Such prayer is one of the twin activities involved in preserving our spiritual lives and helping us to continue to love God until we experience the Lord's mercy in all its fullness when He returns.

All genuine prayer is, I believe, prayer in the Spirit. Without the Holy Spirit, we would not be able to have any fellowship with God the Father at all. He is the channel through which we can communicate with God the Father: *For through him we both have access in one Spirit to the Father* (4). We ask the Father (usually addressing Him) in the name of Jesus (on His authority) in the Holy Spirit (who gives us access). To speak of Him in this way is, of course, not to minimise the personality of the Holy Spirit at all. If we reflect on our best experience of prayer, that certainty of being heard in heaven and even of communion with God that transcends asking for requests to be granted has His distinctive stamp all over it. This is surely communion with the Father and the Son, as enabled by the Spirit.

This is most clearly seen in the fact that in our prayers there is dialogue between the Father and the Spirit. *Likewise the Spirit helps us in our weakness. For we do not know what to pray for as we ought, but the Spirit himself intercedes for us with groanings too deep for words. And he who searches hearts knows what is the mind of the Spirit, because the Spirit intercedes for the saints according to the will of God* (5).

I feel that I have so much yet to learn about prayer although I have been doing it for more than thirty-five years and by God's grace enjoying His presence and His answers. It's no wonder that the disciples pleaded, *"Lord, teach us to pray"* (6). When we think of the difficulty an earwig would have in holding a conversation with us, we can form some conception of why we sometimes find prayer to an infinite and awesome God so difficult. Factor into that the effect of particularly stressful times on our concentration and the difficulty increases even more. We've all experienced times when we want to pray earnestly about a situation and find that we don't even know how to begin expressing ourselves to God about it. How thankful we are then that *the Spirit helps us in our weakness!*

He is so far from being a featureless presence that He *intercedes for us with groanings too deep for words.* The same word is used in Acts 7:34 to describe the groanings of the people of Israel as slaves under their taskmasters. The Calvinist theologian Wayne A. Grudem objects that surely the Holy Spirit would not express Himself to the Father in such terms. Although the Lord Jesus groaned on earth (a similar word to the one translated here as 'groanings' is used in Mk.7:34 to describe our Lord's heavy sigh at the pettiness of His religious opponents), this was because He, unlike the Spirit, had a human nature. Therefore Grudem concludes that the groanings He is helping us with must be ours (7).

The syntax of the sentence (in our English translations at any rate) seems to demand that the groanings are associated with the word 'intercedes', not with the word 'helps', however. They would then be what the Spirit Himself uses in His intercession. The real problem for Grudem isn't in the structure of the sentence, it's that he finds it too baffling that the Holy Spirit Himself should so identify with our afflictions as to use these wordless groans alongside our prayers in helping us. And no wonder! This must surely be one of the deepest examples of the fellowship of the Holy Spirit we can experience here. (Contextually in Rom.8, it is clear that these groanings cannot be equated with the New Testament gift of speaking in tongues.)

Note also that the Spirit has a mind, known to God the Father, showing the fruitfulness of our mind and spirit praying as one. All His intercessions are fully in accordance with the will of God. When we are unsure whether what we might be praying for is the will of God, we can be sure that our Helper in prayer is balancing our ignorance with His knowledge of the divine purpose.

He helps us in the subject matter of our prayers. We can, in our human error, pray for inappropriate things. For example, James gives the example of those who pray for gain to use in satisfying the old nature. *You ask and do not receive, because you ask wrongly, to spend it on your passions* (8).

The famous question in Lk.11:11-12 *("What father among you, if his son asks for a fish, will instead of a fish give him a serpent; or if he asks for an egg, will give him a scorpion?")* suggests that, in our spiritual immaturity, we might sometimes ask for the snakes and scorpions that would do us harm instead of the fish or egg that He wants to give us! Of course, such requests would be withheld by a loving Father.

By contrast, when we pray in the Spirit, He can bring the teaching of the Lord Jesus on prayer to mind, including the 'Lord's prayer' with its guidance. The very opening words, *"Our Father"* are taught by the Spirit. The Spirit of Christ within us teaches us that we can approach Him not only as children but as sons with the full privileges of family: *For you did not receive the spirit of slavery to fall back into fear, but you have received the Spirit of adoption as sons, by whom we cry, "Abba! Father!"* (9). The Saviour gives authority to come making repeated childlike requests for specific things we, or loved ones, may need (10). The prayers of the church in Jerusalem for power in their desperate situation (11) may be one thing He might bring to our recollection whilst on our knees.

Other practical things we are specifically enjoined to pray for by Paul include our governments and peaceful conditions (12); all the saints; and empowerment and clarity for those directly engaged in frontline gospel work (13). Eph.3:14-18 shows a spiritual prayer for deep blessings of spiritual experience that we might desire for ourselves and others. David Woods encouraged us in the last chapter to pray the Word of God and this is surely compatible with praying in the Spirit who inspired it.

Since the first exhortation to pray in the Spirit comes at the end of the description of the armour that God provides for the Christian (14). we can think of it as a weapon in the spiritual warfare. Let's take up arms today to shield us from temptation and weariness and to take God's work forward proactively! Time spent with God getting to know Him is our core business as disciples of the Lord Jesus. Let's enjoy it!

References: (1) Eph.6:18 (2) 1 Cor.14:14-15 (3) see 1 Cor.12:30 (4) Eph.2:18 (5) Rom.8:26-27 (6) Lk.11:1 (7) Systematic Theology (Leicester: Inter-Varsity Press and Grand Rapids: Zondervan 1994), p.1079 (8) Jas.4:3 (9) Rom.8:15; see also Gal.4.6 (10) Lk.11:5-9; Lk.18:1-6 (11) Acts 4:24-31 (12) 1 Tim.2:1-2 (13) Eph.6:18-20, the context in which the phrase 'praying in the Spirit' is used (14) Eph.6:10-20

Bible quotations from the ESV.

1.3 PRAYING ... IN THE NAME (GERALDE MAG-USARA)

Praying in Jesus' name doesn't always mean that these words need to be included in the introduction or at the conclusion of our prayers. Nor does it mean miracles will happen whenever we use those words. The new command to pray in the name of our Lord Jesus was one He emphasized by repetition to His disciples when He was about to go to Calvary:

> *"Whatever you ask in My name, that will I do, so that the Father may he glorified in the Son. If you ask Me anything in My name, I will do it"* (1).

> *"You did not choose Me but I chose you, and appointed you that you would go and bear fruit, and that your fruit would remain, so that whatever you ask of the Father in My name He may give to you"* (2)

> *"... ask the Father for anything in My name, He will give it you ... ask in My name"* (3)

Is there a greater revelation about prayer? Is there a greater challenge to our asking? What does it mean?

The Acknowledgement of Christ as Saviour

Jesus' name (Heb. *Yehshua*) means 'the LORD is salvation' (4). There is no other name in which salvation may be found; only the name of Jesus (5). We become God's children when we believe in His name (6). Our permanent position in Him as our Saviour gives us a confident ground from which to ask things from our heavenly Father. Praying in the name of Jesus acknowledges our position in Him, our Saviour.

Carrying the Sense of Authority and Permission

It also means that He has given us authority as His representatives here on earth. Sometimes when I'm busy, I ask my wife to withdraw money from my bank account through my name. And the bank provides it, not because there's something magical in my name, but its use gives her the authority to represent me and the permission to act for me. It's the same when we pray in Jesus' name. Praying in His name means praying with His authority, believing that God will act because we come in the name of His Son, our Saviour. To prove such authority, it's not always necessary to make a prayer ending with the words "in Jesus' name". When our Lord said, *"Whoever receives one such child in My name receives Me,"* (7) it is entirely possible the situation merely implied the child came at the Lord's bidding, and with His permission.

Later on in the same chapter He said, *"If two of you agree on earth about anything that they may ask, it shall be done for them by My Father who is in heaven. For where two or three have gathered together in My name, I am there in their midst"* (8). The action of clearing a fault between two persons is to take place consciously before the Lord. The asking in that context is not explicitly said to be in Jesus' name, but the gathering is. It's clear that those involved are to deal with the matter by meeting together in these very particular circumstances under the authority of His name.

Relying on His Merit

We come before God's throne of grace, not in our own merit, but in Jesus' merit. It's not about who we are and what we have accomplished when we pray in Jesus' name. Rather it's about who He is and what He has done for us. It's this that permits us to draw near to God through Him. The Father, who is well-pleased with His Son (9) who fulfilled all His will, accepts the requests we make for His sake.

Reflecting His Character in our Asking

It's interesting to read Jesus' prayer, *"I am no longer in the world; and yet they themselves are in the world, and I come to You. Holy Father, keep them in Your name, the name which You have given Me, that they may be one even as We are. While I was with them, I was keeping them in Your name which You have given Me; and I guarded them"* (10). The Lord had told His disciples that He had manifested the Father's name to them during His life. Everything the Lord said and did reflected the values and the character of His Father. His life showed what God was like. Now He prays that the disciples will continue to be kept in that name. In other words, He prays that they will continue to live by the same values that His own example had encouraged them to live by while He was with them. If we are to pray in Jesus' name, then our prayers should reflect Jesus' own values and character.

According to His Will, and Honouring to Him

The Lord's command for us to pray in His name brings with it assurance that He will answer anything we ask that is according to the will of God and that will glorify and honour the Lord Jesus. *This is the confidence which we have before Him, that, if we ask anything according to His will, He hears us. And if we know that He hears us in whatever we ask, we know that we have the requests which we have asked from Him* (11). Praying in Jesus' name means praying according to the will of God. *"Whatever you ask in My name, that will I do, so that the Father may be glorified in the Son. If you ask Me anything in My name, I will do it"* (12). Praying in Jesus' name means requesting things that honour and glorify the Father.

Showing We Are One With Him

Praying in Jesus' name also signifies our legal, living and loving union with God's Son. For the first, we can think of people employed by someone else: what they do is done in the name of the other. The employee who runs a business for his employer, acts in the name of his employer, having had extended to him all the privileges that go with the power of his employer's name, in so far as the business is concerned.

We are in God's kingdom business: to make disciples. We are working for Him, with the assigned task: *"All authority has been given to Me in heaven and on earth. Go therefore and make disciples of all the nations, baptizing them in* [Gk. into] *the name of the Father and the Son and the Holy Spirit, teaching them to observe all that I commanded you"* (13). With this commission had come the words of assurance: *"If you ask Me anything in My name, I will do it"* (14). The apostles immediately applied this: they preached boldly in the name of Jesus (15); healed the sick in the name of Jesus (16); and rebuked evil spirits in the name of Jesus (17).

Second, the union of life: a son bears his father's name, and because he has that name, there belong to him certain privileges. At conversion, we have a new birth status (18) through believing in His name (19). Our position is no longer outside of the family of God. We are joined vitally to the life of God through the new birth. We not only got more privileges when this happened to us, but God *has blessed us with every spiritual blessing in the heavenly places in Christ* (20).

Third, the union of love: a bride takes the name of her bridegroom. The Church which is the body of Christ is described in the Bible as Christ's bride - *having no spot or wrinkle or any such thing* (21). Each of these three aspects of union relate to our new position or status 'in Him' by the grace of God.

Exemplifying our Close Communion

Praying in Jesus' name amounts in practice to the same condition as abiding in 'the vine', the Lord. *"If you abide in Me, and My words abide in you, ask whatever you wish, and it will be done for you ... whatever you ask of the Father in My name He may give to you"* (22). Christian praying is praying in the name of Jesus, in that we approach God, our heavenly Father, on the ground of salvation, and under our Saviour's authority. We pray with His permission, relying only on

His merit. Our requests reflect His character, values and will, so bringing Him honour and glory. It is prayer that grows out from our union with the Lord, and is the fruit of our close communion with Him.

References: (1) Jn 14:13-14 (2) Jn 15:16 (3) Jn 16:23-26 (4) see Matt.1:21 (5) Acts 4:12 (6) Jn 1:12 (7) Matt.18:5 (8) Matt.18:19-20 (9) Matt.3:17 (10) Jn 17:11-12 (11) 1 Jn 5:14-15 (12) Jn 14:13-14 (13) Matt.28:18-20 (14) Jn 14:14 (15) Acts 9:27 (16) Acts 3:6 (17) Acts 16:18 (18) Jn 3:5-7 (19) Jn 1:12 (20) Eph.1:3 (21) Eph.5:27 (22) Jn 15:7,16

Bible quotations from the NASB.

1.4 PRAYING ... IN FAITH AND RIGHTEOUSNESS (ANDY SEDDON)

Praying in Faith

"And whatever you ask in prayer, you will receive, if you have faith" (1).

"Therefore I tell you, whatever you ask in prayer, believe that you have received it, and it will be yours" (2)

These striking words, recorded by Matthew and Mark, were spoken by the Lord Jesus to His disciples in Jerusalem, just a few days before He went to Calvary. It represents a beautiful and challenging promise for all praying Christians, but they are words that could be easily misapplied. Do we really have the right to expect anything from the Lord so long as we 'believe' it will happen? Is Jesus teaching us the power of positive thinking here? Could these words be used to justify the message of the so called 'prosperity gospel'? To correctly understand what Jesus is promising, we address the question, what does it actually mean to 'pray in faith'?

Faith Foundations

Let's say a few opening things about faith itself. First, what is faith? Hebrews defines faith as, *the assurance of things hoped for, the conviction of things not seen* (3). This verse illustrates at a basic level the necessity of faith when we pray, because the very act of prayer is talking to an *invisible God* (4). Second, what is our faith based on? Romans tells us that, *faith comes from hearing, and hearing through the word of Christ* (5). So our faith in prayer must be founded on a correct understanding of who God is, what He is like and what He desires to do. We must never mould God into an image that suits our own taste. No amount of belief, no matter how sincere it is, will prompt God to do something that is inconsistent with His character and will, which He has revealed in His word and through the person of Jesus Christ.

Faith Honours God

Faith in God when we pray honours Him because we are trusting what He says about Himself We are trusting His divine attributes: His omniscience, His omnipotence, His benevolence and His faithfulness. Abraham was commended for his faith; Paul writes about him, *he grew strong in his faith as he gave glory to God, fully convinced that God was able to do what he had promised. That is why his faith was counted to him as righteousness* (6). Note that Abraham's faith was based on what God had already promised, that is based on God's word. The Roman centurion was commended for his faith when he trusted in the supreme authority of the words that Jesus spoke (7). The Lord often commended the faith of those who came to Him for healing.

Ironically, it was often His disciples who were lovingly berated by their master for lacking faith. For example, they failed to trust that He was in control of their lives during the storm on the sea (8), and they were told that the reason they could not heal a boy with a demon was because of their *"little faith"* (9).

Believing is Receiving

The Lord Jesus teaches that we will receive what we ask - if we have faith (10). In contrast, James tells us that the person who doubts, *must not suppose that he will receive anything from the Lord* (11). This is not talking about the strength of positive thinking, but about having confidence in the person to whom we are making the request. We know that in reality we do not possess perfect faith. The Lord's first disciples asked the Lord, *"Increase our faith"* (12) to which Jesus replied, *"if you had faith like a grain of mustard seed"* (13) then they would do things that are only possible for God.

Well-guided Faith

We know that *"with God all things are possible"* (14). However, believing in what God can do must be accompanied by an understanding of what God desires to do, or else our faith is misguided. Who would doubt that God had the power to remove whatever it was that Paul referred to as his 'thorn in the flesh' (15) but, despite Paul's repeated pleadings, God's sovereign wisdom knew that it was in Paul's best interests for the thorn to remain; Paul had to trust that God does what is right, and would give him the grace to cope with this.

There are requests we can make of God which we know without any doubt God will grant us, because we can base it on an unequivocal promise in His revealed Word. For example pursuing wisdom - James declares, *If any of you lacks wisdom, let him ask God who gives generously ... but let him ask in faith* (16). We must also trust God's earnest desire to give us the things He promises. Matthew records how Jesus assured His disciples that our heavenly Father is certain to *"give good things* (or the *"Holy Spirit"* (17)*) to those who ask"* (18).

The Apostle John writes: *And this is the confidence that we have toward him, that if we ask anything according to his will he hears us. And if we know that he hears us in whatever we ask, we know that we have the requests that we have asked of him* (19). Of course, it is not always easy to know what God's will is when it comes to specific issues in our life for which we cannot quote an applicable scripture used in context. In such cases we acknowledge our lack of knowledge as we seek the Holy Spirit's guidance, but without doubting God's power and goodness to do what is right.

Praying in Righteousness

The prayer of a righteous person has great power as it is working (20). Righteousness is faith's guide. Living a righteous life means that our desires will be increasingly tuned to God's desires, and therefore what we ask is more likely to be in accordance with God's will. This is why, *the desire of the righteous will he granted* (21) and *"those who hunger and thirst for righteousness ... shall be satisfied"* (22). The trouble is that we are so often led, not by godly desires, but by selfish and worldly desires, and this will obviously have an impact on our prayer life. James seems to have this in mind when he writes, *"You ask and do not receive, because you ask wrongly, to spend it on your passions"* (23). The remedy is to *Delight yourself in the Lord, and He will give you the desires of your heart* (24).

Sin's Destructive Influence

The negative impact of unaddressed sin should not be understated. The Psalmist was conscious that, *If I had cherished iniquity in my heart, the Lord would not have listened* (25). It is not because sin weakens God's power, but because of the damage that sin does to our fellowship with God. Isaiah writes: *Behold the Lord's hand is not shortened, that it cannot save, or his ear dull, that it cannot hear; but your iniquities have made a separation between you and your God, and your sins have hidden his face from you so that he does not hear* (26).

If we are knowingly tolerating disobedience to God's commands, this must change. When we address this we have a wonderful anticipation of God's mercy and blessing. The apostle John assures us, *Beloved, if our heart does not condemn us, we have confidence before God; and whatever we ask we receive from him, because we keep his commandments and do what pleases him* (27). This is contrasted with a solemn warning in Proverbs that, *If one turns away his ear from hearing the law, even his prayer is an abomination* (28). We are not presuming moral perfection, but rather our attitude towards sin and God's righteousness which is important. When we repent we can be assured of God's mercy; God says: *But this is the one to whom I will look: he who is humble and contrite in spirit and trembles at my word* (29).

References: (1) Matt.21:22 (2) Mk.11:24 (3) Heb.11:1 (4) Col.1:15 (5) Rom.10:17 (6) Rom.4:20-22 (7) See Matt.8:10 (8) See Matt.8:26 (9) Matt.17:20 (10) Matt.21:22 (11) Jas.1:7-8 (12) Lk.17:5 (13) Lk.17:6 (14) Matt.19:26 (15) See 2 Cor.12:7-9 (16) Jas.1:5-6 (17) Lk.11:13 (18) Matt.7:11 (19) 1 Jn 5:14-15 (20) Jas.5:16 (21) Prov.10:24 (22) Matt.5:6 (23) Jas.4:3 (24) Ps.37:4 (25) Ps.66:18 (26) Isa.59:1-2 (27) 1 Jn 3:21-22 (28) Prov.28:9 (29) Isa.66:2

Bible quotations from the ESV.

PART 2 – ABUNDANT BIBLE STUDY

It's absolutely logical that we take a look at Bible study next. As the old Sunday School chorus rightly says: "Read your Bible, pray every day, and you'll grow, grow, grow." However, as with prayer, studying the Bible can be something that we find hard to devote sufficient time to and hard to feel the full benefit of. But it's equally something that we cannot afford to neglect if we want to fully experience who God is and what His purposes are for us in this world.

In our opening chapter of this second segment, Karl Smith emphasises the important role that the heart has to play in our Bible study, which should not simply be an academic exercise; and he also provides some helpful tips on finding your way around the Bible, which is something many people feel intimidated by. In the second chapter, Karl continues by discussing the different types of Bible translations are available and how to interpret the Bible.

This last theme is expanded upon by Brian Johnston in chapter 3, where he gives us 4 very useful pieces of advice in tackling those Bible verses that seem hard to understand, pointing out that although different people may come up with different interpretations of the same Bible verses, we can be sure that there is only one answer that God wants is to search out with His help.

Finally, Martin Archibald concludes this short series with a practical in-depth look at detailed Bible study, and provides a number of checklists that are ideal to put into practice so that the Word of God can take deep root in or hearts and minds and bear abundant fruit in our lives!

2.1 STUDYING WITH YOUR HEART (KARL SMITH)

The most important thing to do with the Bible is to read it! A little time with God's Word every day is an absolute necessity for the Christian who wants to survive as a disciple of the Lord Jesus in this world.

It is also good to sit down and read through the Bible from beginning to end in longer instalments. This gives a sense of perspective as to how the little chunks we read morning by morning fit into the wider picture of the whole Word of God. At least once in your life, you should read the Bible right through from cover to cover. Read another chapter or two in your armchair instead of watching some rubbish on the television that you're not even interested in anyway, on a train or bus journey, while you're having a lie-in, just as you would read any other book. Start at Genesis and go through to Revelation. Only then can you be confident that you've read it all with a sense of the whole narrative.

Once we have gained a broad sense of the Bible's overall narrative, however, it is good to go beyond reading and to study God's Word. Even an hour each week spent looking carefully at the way words are used in the Bible, for example, or the places and people we read about, will really enrich your enjoyment of your normal Bible reading.

The first rule of Bible study is to look for something to obey. Love for the Word of God makes us want to get into it because there we will find His will so that we may do it. God doesn't want us to study just to get more knowledge. He wants us to love Him more and more as we understand more of His ways. We express this love by obeying His commandments. The list of things the Scriptures provide in 2 Tim.3:16-17 concludes with ... *training in righteousness, that the man of God may be complete, equipped for every good work*. If our Bible study is not equipping us to do good for the Master, it is not achieving its purpose.

ABUNDANT CHRISTIANITY

It's not just a head thing – it's a heart thing. We read of one leader amongst God's Old Testament people that *Ezra had set his heart to study the Law of the LORD, and to do it and to teach his statutes and rules in Israel* (1). Ezra's heart was in his Bible study and *the good hand of his God was on him* (2). In response, we read *On the second day the heads of fathers' houses of all the people, with the priests and the Levites, came together to Ezra the scribe in order to study the words of the Law* (3). As a result, they recovered the commandment to keep the feast of tabernacles (or booths), which seems to have been neglected. As they kept this forgotten festival, *there was very great rejoicing* (4).

Our study of the Word of God may bring repentance as we recover neglected truth, but implementing what we have studied in our lives and in our churches leads to real praise to God. Think of those who re-discovered from their study the significance of the simple breaking of bread and of our access into heaven as we gather to remember the Lord Jesus. Think of those who re-discovered the truth about the Lord's coming for believers and His return to rule on earth. Think of those who rediscovered the pattern for the relationship of love and unity between each church of God and for leadership amongst God's people. These joyful discoveries were the result of serious study of the Bible over many generations and we're grateful to each Ezra who set his heart to study, do and teach. Similarly, as we ourselves study we will discover things that the Lord wants to apply to our individual lives and as we do so, there will be repentance and rejoicing.

Bible study will not happen unless we make it happen. You may need to set aside a particular time in the week when you have no other commitments. Finding an hour or two without interruptions can be difficult, especially with family, work and church. Nevertheless, the sacrifice will be rewarded in the here and now. As you dig into the context of each verse, you are digging a well which the Holy Spirit will fill more deeply with joy each time you return to them.

Top tips: The following are some ideas people have shared with me about how to structure a quiet time. Different ones will help different people:

    1. Briefly ask God to help you understand the passage.

2. Don't try to read too much at a sitting.

3. Follow something systematically, such as a book of the Bible.

4. Vary the Old and New Testament in your reading. A reading plan that takes you through the whole Bible in one or more years can be helpful.

5. It might help to read a short passage slowly and more than once so that it sinks in. I personally find this of more value than reading pages and pages.

6. Repeat the words to God, especially ones about Himself, His Son and His Spirit.

7. Look for something about the character of the Lord Jesus to treasure through the day.

8. Look for a command to obey or an example to follow. It may be a negative example to avoid. Above all ask God to help you obey it.

9. Some keep a diary noting in two or three sentences what was in the passage they read.

10. If a phrase or a verse has struck you, memorise it and repeat it to yourself throughout the day.

Finding Your Way Around the Bible

Bible study can take many forms. We may want to follow a character or look up the references to a particular incident. Perhaps we want to find help on a particular aspect of living such as overcoming temptation, relationships or knowing the joy of the Lord. Perhaps we want to find guidance on scriptural teaching affecting aspects of our church life. The person of the Lord Jesus Himself is an especially rewarding subject to research. He Himself is our lovely example and we treasure everything about Him. We will never run short of things to meditate on about Him and this will fuel and enrich our worship too.

The Bible is a big book. If we want to know what the Bible as a whole says about a particular issue, it would take too long to start each time at Genesis 1:1 and go on to Revelation 22:21, stopping each time we came across the subject in which we were interested.

There are, however, tools that can help us here. A concordance, for example, is like a dictionary, but it lists each time every English word is used in the Bible. You can get them for most Bible versions. Before the days of computers, men like Dr James Strong and Robert Young did painstaking work to provide these invaluable tools that are still in use today.

Even these, however, are only a springboard. The Bible might discuss the topic you are interested in without using the particular word for which you happened to search. Say you wanted to study the Lord Jesus' teaching on prayer. Simply looking for 'pray' in a concordance, you might conclude that the Lord's upper room ministry in John 14-16 only speaks about the Lord Jesus praying, but doesn't give any instruction for us. You'd miss out on three or four key passages on the subject, just because the word itself is not used, including such gems as, *Whatever you ask in my name, this I will do, that the Father may be glorified in the Son. If you ask me anything in my name, I will do it* (5). Also a person may be referred to without his or her own name being used.

Many Bibles have cross-references in a column in the middle of each page. A small letter above certain words corresponds to the same letter in the column, where you will see a list of verses. These have been compiled by scholars to point to other key passages where a place or person appears. Sometimes they show other places where broadly the same concept is being dealt with so that we can compare different parts of the Bible by theme. We must, of course, be careful to note differences as well as similarities between verses connected in these ways. The cross-references provide a valuable resource for study inside our Bible editions themselves without turning to lots of reference books. For more extensive help on where to find things, we might invest in a topical (i.e. by topic) dictionary of the Bible or similar book.

Some study tools such as commentaries on particular books, or on the Bible as a whole, give interpretations from Bible students. These can be enormously helpful as we can turn to a verse that is puzzling us and find what others have thought about it. It is worth saying, however, that it is best to study a passage thoroughly yourself before turning to someone else's interpretation. The Holy Spirit has promised to ... *guide you into all the truth* (6) and so we ask that He may do this each time we sit down to reflect on the Scriptures. Even the most scholarly commentaries can consciously or unconsciously reflect the preferences or denominational bias of the writer. Get a range of views rather than reading just one commentator all the time.

References: (1) Ezra 7:10 (2) Ezra 7:9 (3) Neh.8:13 (4) Neh.8:17 (5) John 14:13-14 (6) John 16:13

Bible quotations from the ESV.

2.2 FINDING A BIBLE VERSION AND USING IT (KARL SMITH)

The Bible was not given to us originally in English. The Old Testament, mainly for the people of Israel, was given in their Hebrew language. Some sections in Ezra and Daniel use Aramaic, the dialect the Lord Jesus Himself probably spoke. By the Lord's time, Greek was understood across most of the Mediterranean world, the Romans having taken over the Eastern part of their Empire from the Greeks. God therefore chose this language for the written revelation in the New Testament.

There is then no single 'inspired' English translation of the Scriptures. It is important, however, to choose a version of the Bible that represents the inspired original faithfully. A lot of the study tools you may want to use are based on the Authorised (or King James) Version of 1611, so you may find this beautiful version helpful to use. An update called the New King James Version keeps the old vocabulary where it has not dropped out of use, but uses the grammar of contemporary English to make it easier to follow. Since 1611, more copies of the original manuscripts have come to light and more recent versions take these into account.

I personally like to use a version that aims to put the same English word for the same Greek word throughout, except where this makes the meaning unclear or the context dictates otherwise. The Revised Version aimed to do this and so do its successors, such as the English Standard Version or the New American Standard Bible. This way you can have a fair idea of which Greek word stands behind the English word you are reading. The important thing, however, is that you use a version you can understand.

Some study tools exist to help those of us (including myself) who have not mastered the original languages. An analytical concordance (such as Young's) groups the English words according to the word in the original that they are translating. A lexicon is a special concordance that lists Greek and Hebrew words in alphabetical order instead of English ones. Many computer programmes exist that make all this much easier. You can click on a word in a verse and see straightaway which Greek word it translates and another click will give you all the places that this Greek word occurs! This helps in making connections between verses that we might otherwise miss. For instance, the golden cover of the ark of the covenant with the carved cherubim is translated 'mercy seat' in Heb.9:5, adopting the language of the Old Testament. The Greek word for mercy seat is *hilasterion*. In Rom.3, the word is translated 'propitiation', which means making peace with God, usually by a sacrifice: *Christ Jesus, whom God put forward as a propitiation by his blood, to be received by faith* (Rom.3:24-25 ESV).

Propitiation for the sins of the individual by Christ's death in our place is the subject of Rom.3. When we realise this same word is the New Testament name for the Old Testament mercy seat, where blood was sprinkled annually for the sins of the people, it brings out an interesting linking thought. For a nation of people with sin in their hearts, to approach God would only have brought the judgement of a righteous God, but the shedding and sprinkling of blood in this inner sanctuary is also a 'propitiation' that cleansed everything and allowed them to come near. This was part of the purpose of Christ's sacrifice - to propitiate God so that a New Testament people can enter His presence together and bring sacrifices of praise.

Access to Hebrew and Greek scholarship also helps to recognise subtle distinctions between ideas that a single English word might hide. For example, the Lord's question, "Do you love me?" in Jn 21:15-17, appears to be the same each of the three times in our English translation. Two different words for 'love' appear in the original, however. The first two times, the Lord Jesus asks, "Do you agape me?" (often found as an all-consuming unselfish love of the whole will). Peter replies, "Yes Lord; you know that I phileo you," (usually an affectionate love based on cherishing someone). The third time, the Lord uses Peter's word in the question. Perhaps this suggests that the Lord accepts our phileo, but wants our agape love.

Obviously it is a real advantage to learn these languages or to use the shortcuts outlined above. Please, however, don't be put off studying the Bible if this is not for you. In whatever language, the Lord's requirements of us and the depths of His love become more real to us the more we study the words God uses to convey them to us.

Letting the Bible Interpret Itself

The key to interpreting the Old Testament is the New Testament. Christ fulfilled the Law of Moses and is the saviour Messiah promised through the prophets and celebrated in the Psalms. The study of the Law should have highlighted Israel's need of this Saviour and, as we study it, we can marvel at the beauties of its justice, but also understand our inability to match up to the majestic holiness of God.

This was Paul's experience: *For I delight in the law of God, in my inner being, but I see in my members another law waging war against the law of my mind and making me captive to the law of sin that dwells in my members* (1). This is why he describes it elsewhere as *our schoolmaster to bring us unto Christ* (2). The Pharisees failed in their study of the Scriptures because they would not recognise that Christ was the key to it all. The Lord said to them, *"You search the Scriptures because you think that in them you have eternal life; and it is they that bear witness about me"* (3). Under the guidance of the Holy Spirit, we are unlikely to make the same mistake.

Very often Old Testament Scriptures are quoted in the New. It is always helpful to see what the Lord or the apostles say about a verse from a tricky section of the Old Testament. For example, John looked at the sacrifice of the Lord Jesus on the cross and thought of the Passover lamb.4 The fact that He died before the soldiers came to break His bones, reminded John of the commandment that *...you shall not break any of its bones* (5). This gives a vital clue that the details of the animal sacrifices of the Old Testament reveal aspects of the Lord's sacrificial death on the cross. In the next verse, John quotes Zechariah's prophecy about a time when people would *look on me, on him whom they have pierced* (6). This shows that the person spoken of in this passage is indeed the Lord Jesus.

Later in Rev.1:7 John goes on to apply this to a time to come when others will look on Him with the same sense of awe, perhaps guilt, as the Roman centurion who looked on in Jn 19. With this key in mind, we suddenly understand that the last three chapters of Zechariah explain the realisation among the Jews in a time to come that Jesus was their Messiah after all, giving details about this wonderful turning point in their future that we wouldn't otherwise have.

These - and other texts in the Scriptures - help to explain the large numbers of Israelites faithful to the Lord Jesus in the end times narrated in Revelation. God will take up His purposes with them when the Christians of this age are taken up into heaven. John's quotation of Zechariah also shows that the same prophecy may find its fulfilment in more than one event. The wonder of the Word of God is that these meanings have been contained in it all along and the living person of Christ brings them out. There's not space to develop this here, but for the serious student of future events, a helpful explanation of how to approach the technicalities of prophetic texts can be found in George Prasher's book, 'A study of Prophetic Principles'. Here in the space of two verses in Jn 19, we see how the New Testament illustrated the method of studying both the offerings and of prophecy. The same is true of any other subject we may wish to follow through on.

This unfolding of the Lord's purposes can be seen in our study of the New Testament. The Lord Jesus' words were mainly spoken to Israel and have a special relevance to their national context both then and in the end times. The Gospel writers, however, and the epistles amplify how to apply his teaching in our (mainly Gentile) church age. The Acts show how to spread the Gospel and a model of church growth and structure that are normative for our time. The Epistles show what was - and what was not - desired in individual and church life. Whatever our need, God has provided for it. Moses said of the Law: *it is no empty word for you, but your very life, and by this word you shall live long in the land that you are going over the Jordan to possess* (7). Let's get into it and live by it ourselves.

References: (1) Rom.7:22-23 (2) Gal.3:24 KJV (3) Jn 5:39 (4) Jn 19:36 (5) Ex.12:46 (6) Zech.12:10 (7) Deut.32:47

Bible quotations from the ESV.

2.3 4 KEYS TO UNDERSTANDING YOUR BIBLE (BRIAN JOHNSTON)

1. AVOID THE DANGER OF OVERCOMPLICATING

Understanding how we go about accessing the Bible's true meaning for our lives is the kind of help I could have used very early in my life as a young Christian. I wish someone had encouraged me to read the Bible as you would read any other book - and not as a mysterious text you somehow had to decode using a very specialized skill set.

What added to my struggles was the fact that I listened to preachers who attempted to explain the Bible by saying things like 'this represents that' and so on. The basis for this sort of decoding was seemingly based on what seemed to be random word associations and sometimes what I confess I took to be some rather fanciful notions. A classic historical example of this type of thing comes from a story Jesus told known as the Parable of the Good Samaritan. It concerned a man who had been mugged on a journey. None of his countrymen came to his assistance, but a foreigner did, using his donkey to transport the man to an inn.

Now, in religious history, Augustine suggested the foreigner symbolised Jesus, and the donkey represented the Holy Spirit, as they came to the assistance of the human race. This is an arbitrary spiritual meaning that displaces the actual plain meaning of the words themselves. It treats the plain story as some kind of coded message, and you need to be spiritually tuned in to decode it. Be reassured, Augustine's meaning was not the meaning the Lord intended to convert to his audience that day.

Let me clarify what I've just said – the part about reading the Bible as you would read any other book. Do I mean to say that the Bible isn't special? Of course not. I believe it to be a one of a kind book. It's unique among all books. I hold it to be God's communication to us. For sure, God accommodated himself to human language and employed human authors. But what I mean is this.

Since he used humans and our language, we shouldn't expect the Bible's words to carry something other than their normal plain meanings – at least not unless the Bible itself makes it clear this is to be expected, and then usually it's because of the type of literature it's using at that point. An example would be when there's a clear switch from the standard narrative form to say, a poetic form. No-one should be confused, I hope, if I say the book of Chronicles and the book of Psalms are two different kinds of literature, and we'll naturally find ourselves reading them differently.

Certainly when we're reading the story parts of the Bible, or the letters it contains, we should look for the plain meanings carried by the words in their normal everyday use. And, of course, they follow the ordinary rules of grammar we ourselves follow in everyday communications, usually without thinking about it.

2. GRASP THE IMPORTANCE OF CONTEXT

Another early source of confusion for me came about because I attended 'Bible studies' which consisted of debates about the Bible text where various contributors offered different reconstructions of the particular Bible section in question. Contributors would argue that the dictionary gave one meaning for a particular word of interest; whereas another contributor disagreed by pointing out the same word could have another legitimate meaning. That's when I first learnt the power of context. A particular word can indeed have a variety of meanings, but its use in a specific setting will settle the choice of meaning. Endless debates could have been short-circuited by simply paying more attention to the context than to the dictionary.

A more subtle form of this confusing use of dictionary meanings when applied to words in the Bible concerns the use of Bible dictionaries which drill down to the actual word in the original language rather than its translated equivalent in our modern languages. This does seem more sophisticated and still more so when the dictionary goes on to suggest how the word meanings had supposedly developed over time from their more ancient 'root' or more primitive forms. While this can occasionally be enlightening, it can more often be spurious. Many modern English words have come to us from their roots in the old Latin language, used by the Romans. It's easy to check that it doesn't always follow that the sense of any word as understood today should be influenced by a trace back to its old Latin root word.

So, what are we saying? Simply this: we should read our Bible as we would read any book. The important thing is to be observant. To emphasize the method of understanding a verse by thinking carefully about the verses that come before and after it, we can develop the habit of reading in complete paragraphs or more, and repeatedly reading that larger block of text over and over again until we catch the train of thought.

Memorising verses in isolation can all too easily mislead us when it comes to applying them in our experience. A classic example must surely be Jeremiah 29:11 from where we hear it quoted *I know the plans I have for you says the Lord, plans to prosper you and not to harm you, plans to give you a future and a hope.* Sounds totally reassuring, doesn't it? But this conveniently forgets the historical context of how the words were originally spoken to a disobedient people who were about to be carried away into captivity and judged, long before their descendants would in time – by virtue of this promise – return to resume their normal service. Perhaps we need to be memorising entire paragraphs rather than limited verses, or at least we need to make ourselves aware of the context of the verse we can all too glibly quote.

3. ASK THE RIGHT QUESTIONS

It's an excellent habit when reading the Bible to ask basic questions or the text. 'To whom we this written?' 'And in what specific circumstances?' 'How does their reaction at the time show what they understood the message to be back then?' That last point leads us to what some have settled as the golden rule for working out what a Bible verse means to us today. It's simply this: we shouldn't expect a Bible verse to have a meaning for us that denies whatever it meant to those to whom it was first spoken. To abbreviate that: a verse cannot mean what it never meant (not unless the Bible itself later gives us a fuller expansion).

Let's repeat: meaning is determined by its (literary) context, and words are defined by their contemporary use at the time of writing. Rather than relying on historical searches after older meanings of basic forms of the same word, it's far more likely to be profitable to perform a study of how the word in question was being used by the same Bible author elsewhere in the Bible, or throughout the entire old or new testament, and even in literature of that same time but outside of the Bible.

Mostly, the Holy Spirit used words in the way they were generally used at the time, although it's important to recognise that some important words describe Bible ideas that require us to familiarise ourselves with how the same idea was introduced earlier in the old testament part of the Bible. The safe approach is to compare all other texts related to the one we're reading. For example, the Lord did say on one occasion 'Ask anything in my name and it will be done for you.' However, when we relate this to other teachings about prayer, we find there are indeed conditions that are meant to be understood - they're taken as read in that instance, and involved implicitly in what it truly means to ask in our Lord's name.

4. REMEMBER THAT THERE IS ONLY ONE 'RIGHT ANSWER'

It's worth saying that we live in an age where truth has become devalued. Absolute truth is denied. What's true for you may be irreconcilably different from what's true for me, or so some say. That position, however, amounts to a denial of the God of truth and of God's Word of truth, the Bible. It leads some to say that there are many possible interpretations of any single Bible verse. Take your pick, whatever works for you, they tell us. This is definitely not the way to understand the Bible. There is one correct way to interpret every single Bible verse – even if we at times struggle to grasp it. Do we think God is incapable of expressing himself clearly? No, our Lord explained certain Bible verses as critically depending on a word being singular rather than plural, and in another case the true meaning depended on the tense of the verb. Such precision falsifies the idea that what was conveyed was flexible enough to bear practically any meaning we might choose for it.

How then can we be sure we've found the correct meaning of any disputed text? The answer to that expands on the idea of context that we were talking about earlier. I well remember a Christmas-time when my daughter was small. One of her presents was a jigsaw puzzle. In other words, a puzzle comprised of many pieces of a picture, all of them cut into different shapes. When correctly assembled, together they formed a coherent picture – in this case it was a picture of a black Labrador dog. The problem was I had thrown away the packaging which contained the only reference picture of the dog - which picture we needed to follow as our guide! This made the puzzle more challenging than it should've been. Verses of the Bible can be compared to those puzzle pieces. But when through cover to cover reading, we build up a sense of where the bigger picture, the meta-narrative of the Bible, is headed, we then have that as our guiding picture for how we get the unique meaning of the individual verses including the difficult or obscure ones.

2.4 AN INTRODUCTION TO SYSTEMATIC BIBLE STUDY (MARTIN ARCHIBALD)

Is Study for Every Bible Reader?

From Bible study, Daniel worked out the year of release from captivity. From their study, we judge Simeon and Anna knew that Christ would come to the Temple in their lifetime, and so were there to hold Him as a baby in their arms. A Temple-poet was so deeply impressed at what he gained from the words of God that he wrote a poem of 176 beautifully patterned verses about his meditation. For reasons like these J.C. Ryle, preacher and theologian, said, "We must read our Bible like men digging for hidden treasure." That is, we will be enriched beyond measure if we read with single-minded, untiring devotion, as of those who search deeply, and find wonderful things.

But is systematic Bible study a rewarding aim for every disciple? Is it not enough to read a chapter a day? I think our personal answer will depend on what success we have in that daily reading. If we have met *God* in His Word, will we not wish to listen more for His voice, and understand what He says more clearly? Of if we have not yet managed to find Christ "in *all* the Scriptures", are we not drawn to do even a little more searching for how those other parts testify of Him? We may remember also that the Jews in Beroea were commended for the strength of character they showed in "*examining* the Scriptures daily." If daily reading is working properly, it will leave an urge to follow up a topic or inquiry through a book, or Bible-wide, whether we are naturally studious and do so intensively, or are ordinary readers, and take a quieter pace. Certainly, study will speed our progress from "milk" to "solid food" (Heb.5:12-14), provided we strive to practise what we find.

Study is also the safeguard against the natural inclination to build on a verse or passage isolated from its setting, and thereby give it a false meaning. For example, the Lord advised His disciples when witnessing to kings and governors.

> *... not to meditate beforehand how to answer for I will give you a mouth and wisdom, which all your adversaries shall not be able to withstand or gainsay* (Lk.21:14,15).

Someone might regard this as an instruction not to prepare for giving a Gospel address or a talk to youth—and find no such help forthcoming! Whereas a careful study of the setting shows it belongs to times of extreme persecution when there would be little freedom to consult a Bible, or time free of harassment, and the need to speak in a position of intense pressure. The student finds also in his wider reading that even in the Old Testament, the advice of the book entitled 'Preacher' (see Eccles.12:9,10) is different, because the context there is a prepared lesson or address. Again, Peter says for everyday witnessing, *being ready always to give answer to everyman that asketh you a reason concerning the hope that is in you* (1 Pet.3:15 RV).

The same danger arises on a broader front, since the outlook of a whole Bible book needs to be compared with the teaching on its subject found in other books. Ecclesiastes, for instance, deals with life as observed naturally "under the sun", that is, its view at many points is that of human wisdom, recording with devastating power the message of disillusionment with the passing pleasures of this life. There are certain points (e.g. Eccles.5:19,20; Eccles.12:1) at which the reader is guided to a deeper spiritual understanding that teaches us to ask for God's help in finding the meaning of life. But when Ecclesiastes has taught us not to trust in this world's prosperity, we are almost forced to take refuge in a neighbouring book like the Psalms to seek more of God's answer to our spiritual need.

Thus we do well to undertake Bible *study* to gain a balanced overview of any Scriptural subject, tracing it through the Old Testament into the New. Further support for this point may be seen in 1 Cor.10:6,11.

Finding Time

A little study is of course better than none, but an hour snatched at random in the week will not take us far, and an isolated burst of lengthy study will likely make us put off the next spell for as long as possible. Any study benefits greatly if we reserve time regularly for it. Some may be able to keep, say, a particular night in the week for this, sometimes using it to prepare for an address or class (though likely finding that some further hours have to be worked in somewhere). But when beginning a family, or changing jobs upsets the routine, it will prove well worth the effort to defend at least an hour or two each week for deepening our knowledge of the ways of God. (And I *have* heard this said by young mothers!) *Unless Thy law had been my delight, I should then have perished in my affliction* (Ps.119:92, NIV). When study becomes hard exercise, it can be helpful to ensure that something relaxing or easier to enjoy is worked into the timetable afterwards, rather than give up in discouragement.

It will of course be time well spent to begin with prayer for the Holy Spirit's teaching. This helps us to recognize the positive action that should flow from any study of the living Word, whether to adjust our inward attitudes, or to take some outward action like settling an old disagreement, or setting ourselves some goal in service. It helps also to continue to ask for the Spirit's leading as we come up against a difficult problem—or find things flowing with suspicious ease!

Prayerful meditation avoids:

1. strengthening our own prejudices;

2. hiding from unpleasant truths;

3. pursuing 'pet' themes only;

4. developing blind spots in familiar passages;

5. giving up when a passage become obscure.

Where to Begin

From the range of possible approaches, perhaps the most immediately attractive one would be the character-study. This is as inviting as the opportunity to meet a new friend (or even to learn from someone who was a failure!), or to get to know an acquaintance more deeply. We can develop an exciting sense of spiritual companionship, while we learn from God's dealings with the person. We are free to choose from the Old Testament or New; and if from Old, we may in most cases look forward to seeing how the New provides the best commentary of all.

Here is a simple plan of inquiry:

(a) Background circumstances.

(b) Life before God's first 'dealing'.

(c) The effects of the first personal experience of God.

(d) God's purpose and work for the character.

(e) Qualities of character formed; weaknesses overcome? e.g. were this person's natural abilities used notably by God after conversion or calling?

(f) Influence on others.

(g) Failures and successes, and the reasons for them.

We might then try a Book-study, which has several attractive features. We can choose from a range of lengths; a range of difficulty; and according to the likely relevance to our current circumstances. Again, we may choose from Old Testament or New. It would be wise, however, to look for an outline guide if we are 'beginners', such as those provided in the Scofield Bible, or the NIV Study Bible. Better still would be to ask an older brother or sister to work with you or advise—fruitful in friendship as well as learning! More experienced students will enjoy working out their own summary-outline as they go along, and adjusting its shortcomings as understanding matures.

One of the Gospels always makes a profitable beginning, and will lead us sooner or later to comparison with the other three. A book like Romans or Galatians, however, will yield most if we already know the Old Testament books of the

Law quite well, e.g. from having read them more than once in daily reading, since we will not appreciate the Jewish veneration of the Law unless we have come to value its richness ourselves.

Other Types of Study

Now we might choose from a more demanding range: of theme or topic; a word-study; some of the Old Testament types of Christ; or prophecy.

For a theme-study, which in theory could lead us through all 66 books, we would be wise to choose a group of books, e.g. the books of Moses, to give practical limits; or follow, for example, personal holiness through a sample-book from each of: the Law, the histories (Ruth to Esther), the poetic books, the prophets; a Gospel, the Acts, a Letter by Paul, and a non-Pauline Letter. This would of course be a study in quite some depth! A lighter course might follow 'holiness' and 'sanctification' and related words through the Concordance, selecting only the occurrences that are likely to illustrate a distinct aspect.

What we are looking for here is the flavour that belongs to a particular Hebrew or Greek word, compared with its synonyms. Each carries its own subtle (or more marked) variations of sense, and this can be used with special effect by the Holy Spirit's guidance of the writer. For instance, Romans 10:17 says, *So belief comes from hearing the message, and the message is heard through the word of Christ*. Here the Greek translated 'word' is 'rheuma', which is used in the New Testament for the spoken word especially, reminding us of the necessity for oral witness and preaching.

Our method would be to choose a passage where, for example, the word 'power' occurs more than once, and find 'power' in the concordance list of all occurrences of a Greek word that is translated with that English word. We might first profit from looking at the range of verses where the English 'power' translates the Greek dunamis = ability, compared with those where 'power' translates exousia = authority, and noting how this affects our understanding of the passage we first chose.

Then we could look at other English words used to translate dunamis elsewhere. For this, turn to the list of Greek words near the end of Dr Young's concordance, which is the best for this kind of inquiry.

Here is part of the list:

ability 1

might 4

miracle 8

virtue 3

The figure shows the number of times dunamis is translated by the English word in the A.V. It is interesting to note the eight places where the translation is 'miracle'; though as we would expect, the commonest rendering is 'power' (77 times). If 'virtue' drew our attention, we would benefit from looking at its derivation in our English dictionary, where we'd find it once was nearer to its original sense in Latin, viz. 'power' or 'strength'. We need hardly add that, with prayer, such an inquiry should result in fresh light from the Word that would enrich our worship, prayer, witness and fellowship.

Another exacting but fruitful search is *the types of Christ* to be found in the Old Testament. This ranges from characters like Joseph, to the provisions of the Law, where Christ and His work is seen in the service of the priesthood, and in sacrifice and offering. We may search the material structure of the dwelling-places of God on earth among His people for pictures of Christ as Son over God's house today; and the imagery of the prophets, such as *the shadow of a mighty rock in a weary land*. For the types form one of the richest sources of finding Christ "in all the Scriptures". Nor should we miss the treasury of the poetic books, with their description of the sufferings of the Lord, and the glories that should follow.

To finish this brief sketch of a large field, we note the importance of recognizing possibly four distinct layers of truth here:

(1) the immediate meaning of the Old Testament text for the time in which it was first written;

(2) the fulfilment of prophecy for Israel in the days of the Lord's first coming, and perhaps also for the Gentiles;

(3) elements of prophecy that concern Israel as a nation for which God still has unique purposes;

(4) elements that are related directly to New Testament believers, in Christ, and to His gathered together people.

There is general agreement that (3) is the largest single element in prophecy.

Lastly, we observe that one passage can contain all four layers, some of which have already been fulfilled, e.g. Isa.9:1-7, where we read (1) of the eventual defeat of Assyria (vv.4,5); (2) the birth of the Messiah (3) His millennial reign (4) the kingdom of God and of His Christ in eternity (v.7b).

Essential Questions for Every Passage

Now to draw up a 'plan of attack' that will keep us on profitable lines in any area of the Bible. We suggest five main questions.

(1) *What did this passage mean to the writer or speaker and to his first audience?* The more we dig in this direction, the more we will be consulting language dictionaries, and works on the history of Bible times, and historical geography. Two cautions may help. First, beware of assuming that the vegetation and wildlife of Israel today is identical to that of Bible times. Rivers may also change their course through history, and between summer and winter! Second, while the archaeology and mapping of ancient Israel is a fascinating study, there are a large number of places that cannot be identified with certainty by scholars. Therefore we conclude that the meanings of Bible names are often more important, and carry far more spiritual profit, than working out their location on a map. We can also usefully subdivide this question with the old battery of guns, "Who, What, Where, When and Why?"

(2) *Make a list of the main points in the passage.* This will keep in mind the overall structure the writer is developing, and help us find our way more quickly when we return to the chapter later. Good for memory too!

(3) *Have I found Christ reflected in the concerns of this passage?* One route to meditation on our Lord is to ask in what way the topics of our passage would interest *Him*.

(4) *What is the relevance of this portion today?* Essential stimulus to spiritual growth and *action*.

(5) *Where is this verse or passage commented on elsewhere in the Scriptures?* The best commentary of all, as we noted above. "Nothing can cut the diamond but diamond; nothing can interpret Scripture but Scripture." (Thomas Watson). Scholars today still say that the next best is the marginal references of the Revised Version.

The five questions will take time, but will yield the fruits of thoroughness, that Martin Luther spoke of: "Pause at every verse of Scripture and shake, as it were, every bough of it, that if possible some fruit may at least drop down."

Helpful Checks

For the last lap, here is a bank of profitable checks on our findings.

(1) If the Spirit caused so many more pages to be occupied with the *Old Testament* books, let us not miss the value of looking there for the foundations of God's treatment of any subject. Brethren have also long taught the worth of studying especially the *first mention* of a topic. In general, the book of Genesis offers a very important field for beginning our study.

(2) A great deal can be gained by comparing modern with older translations. It is still true, however, that the Revised Version offers the most consistent use of English words to translate the original equivalents, and so gives directness to our study. It also tends to avoid simplifying a Greek expression in order to make it easily recognisable to modern or Western readers. For example, "the church of the Thessalonians in God the Father" is a richer concept than the easier

rendering (Revised English Bible) suggests. Following the Revised Version use of English renderings usually yields rapid access to key passages on a chosen subject. But modern translations can often force us to look especially at familiar portions with fresh eyes.

(3) It is essential to observe the rule of faithfulness to *the context* or setting of a word or verse. This will help us, for instance, to distinguish between the imagery of building up the Church the Body of Christ from building in the house of God.

The Lord Bless Your Search

So there are some guidelines that our spiritual fathers have commended to us. Let the words of the veteran of preaching and teaching urge us on: "Do your best to present yourself to God as one approved, a workman who does not need to be ashamed and who correctly handles the word of truth."

PART 3 – ABUNDANT CHURCH LIFE

It should be extremely clear from a reading of the New Testament that God does not intend for us to live for Him simply as individual disciples – He wants us to serve Him in conjunction with other believers.

However, modern church life is not without its significant problems. There are hundreds of different denominations with widely varying beliefs and practices – how can we be sure what is the Biblical model or pattern for church life? Secondly, many Christians seem dissatisfied and disillusioned with their church lives and some fall into the trap of flitting around from church to church, and some stop going to church altogether. What are the key attributes of a church that will help prevent that? This third segment of the book provides assistance on both these challenges.

James Needham starts off this mini-series by emphasising that importance of collective learning in the church community, based solidly of course on the Word of God, not the ideas of man. Steve Seddon then looks at the immense value of church fellowship, drilling down into what it provided and what is needed for it to function properly.

In chapter three, Craig Jones reminds us that worship should be absolutely essential and central to the life of the church and should be characterised by warmth and life, not cold formality! Finally, Brian Johnston looks at the vital subject of collective prayer. As he points out, prayer is not meant to be an individual pursuit, and the New Testament record gives examples of this, and we need to appreciate that God views a collecting praying people as something that's very special to Him.

May these chapters help propel us to more fruitful and abundant service together.

3.1 COLLECTIVE LEARNING THAT LIVES (JAMES NEEDHAM)

On the morning of the day of Pentecost, 50 days after the Lord Jesus had risen from the dead, the unveiling of God's purposes for the present age advanced in mighty power. Sin and death had been vanquished on the cross outside Jerusalem, and now within its walls the first bright rays of the day of grace shone with unbridled glory as the Holy Spirit descended from heaven to clothe the disciples *with power from on high* (1).

On that day alone, three thousand people were joined with the 120 who had been waiting in Jerusalem in response to their Lord's command. By salvation, baptism and addition (2), they became fellows, not of an inert society, but a vibrant community whose purpose was, in their worship and their walk, to *proclaim the excellencies of him who called [them] out of darkness into his marvelous light* (3). Their addition to this community was just the beginning of a life of discipleship, in which God would disclose to them the fullness of His nature and the richness of the purposes conceived in His mind. So, from that day onwards, as a vital part of their development as followers of Christ, *they devoted themselves to the apostles' teaching* (4).

Its Origin

This reference to the apostles' teaching describes the whole body of doctrine which was delivered to the first Christians by the apostles and, although it bears their name, it came from a source which was far higher than they. This is attested by Peter, years after that first gospel address, as he told those united with him by faith that *no prophecy was ever produced by the will of man, but men spoke from God as they were carried along by the Holy Spirit* (5).

Even the teaching of the Lord Jesus Himself, which He delivered with unparalleled authority, had its origin in God the Father. Coming to the Temple during the feast of John 7, He answered those who were amazed at Him, *my teaching is not mine, but his who sent me* (6). As the Father commanded Him, so He spoke in the power of the Spirit (7). This continued during the forty days which followed the resurrection, as He equipped the apostles for their task with lessons about the kingdom of God. So all that the Lord had passed to them through the Holy Spirit, they were now to pass to others as the Spirit guided their understanding, for this was the ultimate purpose of His final commandment before returning to heaven: *make disciples of all nations … teaching them to observe all that I have commanded you* (8).

What then, about Paul, who was not among the 120 people who were empowered by the Holy Spirit on the day of Pentecost? Well, he too received his instruction from God (9). Despite his education in the Scriptures (10), Paul made no pretence that his teaching was the product of his own mind: *I did not receive it from any man, nor was I taught it, but I received it through a revelation of Jesus Christ* (11). So whether it was taught by 'the Eleven' or imparted by those called to apostleship much later, this teaching came from God Himself, delivered to the apostles by the Lord through the Holy Spirit, that they might establish its place at the heart of the community God had made for Himself on earth. Though it bore their name, this was always *the teaching of Christ* (12), declared by the Spirit to the churches (13), and acknowledged in the world as *the teaching of the Lord* (14).

Its Certainty

Since this teaching has been delivered by the Lord through the work of the Holy Spirit, we can be sure it has been conveyed with accuracy, for God always watches over His word (15). By the time of Jude's letter, it had also been conveyed completely, as he appealed to those who had been called to *contend for the faith that was once for all delivered to the saints* (16). As to fundamental principles, nothing could be added to it, and nothing taken away, for that which had been *declared at first by the Lord, and … attested to us by those who heard* (17) was complete in every respect, and the responsibility of disciples of Christ was to contend earnestly for it.

Those days were no different from today, as the sound doctrine of God came under assault from false teachers, and those who sought to undermine it by division (18). Today, as then, the teaching of men must be measured by the standard of that which has been delivered *once for all* by the Lord through the apostles. The Scriptures declare this is a *trustworthy word* (19), made sure in the purposes of God and able to withstand every assault.

This certainty was reflected in the consistency with which the apostles taught it throughout the churches of God. Though they were spread across continents, the apostles' teaching was like a cast, designed to achieve the same result wherever it was applied. That is the meaning of Paul's words to the Romans, as he rejoiced that they had *become obedient from the heart to the standard of teaching to which you were committed* (20). 'Standard' literally means a 'mould' into which the Roman disciples had been poured that it might set the shape of their lives. What was true for them was true for Timothy, whom Paul encouraged in *the pattern of the sound words* (21). So whether the teaching was imparted to a congregation in Rome, or to an individual in his own service, the impression must be the same, for the pattern they were to imitate produces no other result. They were to learn *my ways in Christ, as I teach them everywhere in every church* (22) - departure from them was departure from the teaching of the Lord Himself.

Its Purpose and Effect

Set against this background of the completeness and certainty of the teaching which God has prescribed for our day, it remains essential to recognise that this is a teaching which must be lived in the lives of disciples. Adherence is not achieved by amassing knowledge, nor by engaging in ritual performance - far from it! This is the blueprint for living in the image of Christ and the means by which disciples are led in an ever-deepening understanding of God and His ways. It is by the apostles' teaching that the Holy Spirit makes known to us the *secret and hidden wisdom of God, which God decreed before the ages for our glory* (23), and by it that God establishes the terms of His covenant relationship with a called-out people sprinkled by blood for obedience to the book, as Israel once had been at Sinai (24). So this teaching is far from dusty head-knowledge - it is the unveiling of truths which have delighted the heart of God for eternity, that by them we might grow in our knowledge of Him and our appreciation of all His purposes for us in divine service (25).

That kind of teaching is transformative, for teaching which gleans from the mind and heart of God must have its effect in ours. It did for the Romans. Having been poured into its mould, they who once had been *slaves of sin* became *slaves to righteousness leading to sanctification* (26). It completely changed the character of their lives! Today, many would scoff at the simplicity and purity of living which Paul describes as the character of those who live out the apostles' teaching (27). And yet, by living in conformity with the *sound doctrine,* they are described by the Spirit as *adorning the doctrine of God our Saviour.* How wonderful that God should consider those who display the vitality of His teaching as adorning it with beauty! That's the purpose, of course: that this teaching should so affect our lives as to change us forever; to become more like the Master we serve and, by living in faithfulness to the *word of Christ,* so adorn the doctrine of God.

References: (1) Lk.24:49 (2) Acts 2:41 (3) 1 Pet.2:9 (4) Acts 2:42 (5) 2 Pet.1:16,20-21 (6) Jn 7:16 (7) Jn 12:49-50; Acts 1:2 (8) Matt.28:19-20 (9) 1 Cor.11:23;15:3 (10) Phil.3:5-6 (11) Gal.1:12 (12) 2 Jn 9 (13) c.f. Rev.2:7 (14) Acts 13:12 (15) Jer.1:12 (16) Jude 1:3 (17) Heb.2:3 (18) Rom.16:17-18 (19) Tit.1:9 (20) Rom.6:17 (21) 2 Tim.1:13 (22) 1 Cor.4:17 (23)1 Cor.2:7 (24) Heb.9:19-20; 1 Pet.1:2 (25) Eph.3:14-19 (26) Rom.6:17-19 (27) Tit.2:1-10

Bible quotations from the ESV.

3.2 COLLECTIVE FELLOWSHIP THAT FUNCTIONS (STEVE SEDDON)

Second on the list of the four activities that characterised the first church of God, fellowship is up there as a priority set by God for His people. But what is fellowship, and what does being 'devoted' (1) to it look like?

With limited application in contemporary English, we must turn to the original Greek, *koinonia*. A brief look at what is embodied in the meaning of the word, coupled with a contextual review of key occurrences in scripture, reveals a multi-facetted gem: a doctrine, whose origin and perfect example belong with God Himself, but which also finds its expression in relationships within a church of God, of a kind that are necessary if that church is to be the functioning fellowship that God intends.

Glimpse the Ideal

Fellowship that functions is demonstrated in the perfect community that is the mystery of a triune God: three divine persons of equal rank, being one God, forming a relationship perfect in love, unity, function and purpose:

- The Father loves the Son and gives Him everything (2).

- The Son loves the Father and always does what pleases Him (3).

- The Spirit takes the things of the Son and shows them to us, and glorifies the Son in the process (4).

But what of fellowship in a church of God? It may not be possible to arrive at a single statement that spans the full meaning of the word, but here's an attempt that hopefully will encourage our thinking towards a more expansive appreciation of the doctrine behind the word and how it applies to disciples in churches of God today: Fellowship *[koinonia]* implies a common bond that connects disciples together (with each other and with God Himself) and yields a deep and profound relationship characterised by holiness, unity, and affection - for the accomplishment of God's will and purposes, bringing honour to Him and joy and fulfilment to everyone involved.

Vertical and Horizontal

We proclaim to you what we have seen and heard, so that you also may have fellowship with us. And our fellowship is with the Father and with his Son, Jesus Christ (5). John here describes an activity which happens in two dimensions:

- At a horizontal level between fellow disciples of the Lord Jesus
- At a vertical level between those disciples and with the Father and with His Son, Jesus Christ.

These essential vertical and horizontal elements lay the foundation for our fuller understanding of what else is involved in fellowship that functions, and our devotion to it.

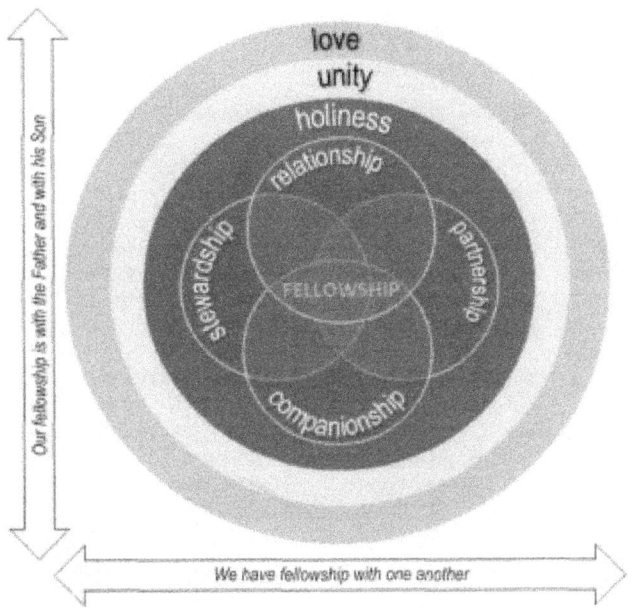

Holiness, the Essential Prerequisite

In his first epistle, John confirms an inextricable link between properly functioning fellowship and the purity of those doing it: *If we claim to have fellowship with [God] yet walk in the darkness, we lie and do not live by the truth. But if we walk in the light, as he is in the light, we have fellowship with one another, and the blood of Jesus, his Son, purifies us from all sin. If we claim to be without sin, we deceive ourselves and the truth is not in us. If we confess our sins, he is faithful and just and will forgive us our sins and purify us from all unrighteousness* (6).

Holiness is at the core of fellowship that functions. Rather than being a consequence of fellowship, it is an essential prerequisite. There is an individual and collective responsibility for holiness in the context of fellowship. There is no room for unconfessed sin - be that intentional or unintentional sin committed by individuals. And there can be no room for hidden sin - even turning a blind eye to the unconfessed sins of others, leaving the dealing of their sin to their own conscience. Mercifully, we have a faithful God who is eager to forgive, and once we have known His forgiveness, surely the result, by the indwelling Holy Spirit, is a heightened sensitivity to sin that will lead to holiness and commitment to personal purity. Fellowship without forgiveness is flawed and dysfunctional.

Four Facets of Fellowship

1. Relationship

Implicit in all that we have said so far is that fellowship is a collective activity. It requires healthy relationships between disciples, and that those disciples in a collective sense, have a healthy relationship with God the Father and the Lord Jesus. The vertical aspect of fellowship makes it distinctive from what would otherwise be ordinary relationships that people, regardless of any common faith, can have with each other. For example, family members spending time enjoying each other's company, or a group of people with a common interest getting together to share their interest. Neither of these could be described as Christian fellowship. A family enjoys family-time; Christians, because of their relationship with God, enjoy fellowship.

2. Partnership

For fellowship to be functional, it must be productive. This is about disciples serving together as partners towards a God-given common purpose, and achieving it. The concept of disciples living and working together in harmony in order to be effective in their service is at the heart of the writings of the apostles to the first century churches of God. Paul shows his great appreciation for this aspect of the fellowship he had with those in the Church of God in Philippi. *In all my prayers for all of you, I always pray with joy because of your partnership in the gospel from the first day until now, being confident of this, that he who began a good work in you will carry it on to completion until the day of Christ Jesus* (7).

3. Companionship

The apostle John describes himself as *your brother and companion* [Gk. akin to *koinonia*] *in the suffering and kingdom and patient endurance that are ours in Jesus.8* By describing himself in this way, we get a sense of the mutual commitment he and his fellows had made to God and to each other. They were in it together, for the duration, not to be deterred by prevailing difficult circumstances. The fact of his writing to his companions is, in itself, an evidence of fellowship in action. No doubt those on the receiving end of his letter would have been excited by its arrival and keen to understand and embrace its content.

4. Stewardship

Stewardship is the practical business of caring and sharing that very clearly characterised the first church in Jerusalem where, *All the believers were together and had everything in common. Selling their possessions and goods, they gave to anyone as he had need 9* This is beautifully illustrated by the fellowship Paul celebrated in his letter to the Philippians: *it was good of you to share in my troubles ... when I was in Thessalonica, you sent me aid again and again when I was in need ... I am amply supplied, now that I have received...the gifts you sent. They are a fragrant offering, an acceptable sacrifice, pleasing to God* (10) - an intensely practical aspect of true fellowship. When these elements of human interaction are set in the context of a lively collective relationship with a holy and loving God, with a commitment to personal and collective purity, wonderful things happen:

Unity

It is unthinkable that any group engaging in the kind of fellowship we have described could do so if they were at odds with each other. The Lord Jesus Himself in His prayer for the future generations that would believe in Him alludes to a beautiful interconnected functioning fellowship that cultivates unity: *... that all of them may be one, Father, just as you are in me and I am in you. May they also be in us ... they may be one as we are one: I in them and you in me. May they be brought to complete unity* (11). Fellowship that functions cultivates unity, and unity is delightful - delightful to those doing it, and a delight to God Himself. *How good and pleasant it is when brothers live together in unity! ... For there the Lord bestows his blessing, even life for evermore* (12).

Love

Love here is more specifically 'brotherly affection'. *Be devoted to one another in brotherly love. Honour one another above yourselves. Never be lacking in zeal, but keep your spiritual fervour, serving the Lord. Be joyful in hope, patient in affliction, faithful in prayer. Share with God's people who are in need. Practise hospitality* (13). Paul's exhortation to the Romans seems to embrace all the aspects of fellowship we have considered, but includes an instruction towards love. Experience shows that love is not something to be turned on at a whim - it can only happen as a consequence of the gracious work of the Holy Spirit over time as we engage with our brothers and sisters. Put another way, like unity, love is an inevitable consequence of properly functioning fellowship.

Fake or fulfilling?

We are designed to enjoy fellowship that functions - it is the route to a fulfilled life that can be matched by no other. Our challenge before the Lord is to examine the quality of our devotion to fellowship, and to seek by His enabling to embrace every aspect of it - together.

References: (1) Acts 2:42 (2) Lk.10:22 (3) Jn 4:34 (4) Jn 16:14 (5) 1 Jn 1:3 (6) 1 Jn 1:6-9 (7) Phil.1:4-6 (8) Rev.1:9 (9) Acts 2:44-45 (10) Phil.4:14-18 (11) Jn 17:21-23 (12) Ps.133 (13) Rom.12:10-13

Bible quotations from the NIV (1984).

3.3 COLLECTIVE WORSHIP THAT WARMS (CRAIG JONES)

Over 20 years ago, a small group of us led a young people's weekend retreat in the English Lake District, at which we considered the subject of 'worship'. We asked the young people to form small groups and to discuss what they thought 'worship' actually meant. From the feedback we received, we then agreed, as a group, on a definition, which was: 'Worship is the expression of the realization of who we are before God.' That's not a bad definition. However, I might be inclined to modify it slightly to say that 'worship is the expression of our realization of who God is.' The Oxford English Dictionary has it: 'The feeling or expression of reverence and adoration for a deity.' For Christians, of course, that deity is the one true God of heaven and earth - the only person to whom worship should be given (1)!

Throughout the generations since the early churches of God of the New Testament, many forms of worship to God have developed, with varying degrees of ritual and ceremony. We might justifiably wonder what God gets from all this diversity (and in some cases contradiction) of practice, and to what extent the principle of 'good, better and best' might apply. If it's an appropriate question to be exercised about - and God's precision in specifying how the Israelites were to worship and serve Him strongly suggests that it is - then it's good to look at what the early churches of believers in the Lord did and to seek to emulate that example of authentic, collective Christian worship today.

Acts 2:41-42 are often pointed to as, effectively, an executive summary, or prescription, of the core activities to which the first church of God in Jerusalem *were continually devoting themselves*. The service and worship of those first local churches of Christian believers revolved around these important activities, which must have become defining hallmarks of the first-century community of believers in the Lord Jesus.

It's no surprise, either, to find the 'breaking of the bread' featuring as one of those important core activities, which together constitute expressions of worship of the church. The simple format of that memorial commemoration, involving broken bread and poured-out wine individually distributed to the gathered disciples, was given by the Lord Himself in an upper room, when He commanded His disciples to *"do this in remembrance of Me"* (2). On that fateful night, when we would think that the mind of the Lord could so easily have been distracted by so many unsettling thoughts about what was soon to happen to Him, with loving forethought and clarity of mind, He gave this simple, yet profound, ordinance to those whom He had called, and whom He loved to the uttermost, as an ongoing reminder of all that He was about to do for them - and indeed for us also! Paul received the very same instructions concerning the simplicity of that remembrance by direct revelation from the Lord Jesus Himself (3).

In their accounts of the events of that evening, both Matthew and Mark record for us that, after the Lord had instituted the remembrance, they sang a hymn (4). How wonderfully appropriate now, too, that such a profound, poignant and touching commemoration of the sacrifice of the Lord Jesus should be followed by a joint singing of praise, as a heartfelt, collective response and expression of worship! In fact Paul, in his lengthy and instructive teaching to the Church of God in Corinth about the order and format of church gatherings, specifically mentions psalms as one of the elements included when the church gathered for worship (5). The speaking of psalms, hymns and spiritual songs (6) was also encouraged by Paul as a means for believers to exhort one another in their daily faith, and so replicating that practice in their collective experience of sung worship as a church was both natural and appropriate.

We also observe in Paul's teaching to the church in Corinth, that expressions of praise to God by the brothers in the church were part of that particular collective worship experience (7). This resonates wonderfully with the encouragement of Heb.13:15, for us to *continually offer up a sacrifice of praise to God, that is, the fruit of lips that give thanks to His name.* Sacrifices of praise articulated in these ways - audibly by the brothers and silently by the sisters - constitute the *spiritual sacrifices acceptable to God through Jesus Christ* (8) which are the willing obligation of those *living stones* whom the Lord constitutes *a spiritual house for a holy priesthood* (9).

So then, if all that speaks largely of the format and procedure of that aspect of the collective worship of a biblical church of God, what of the substance, the content? It's instructive for us to appreciate, even on a simple level, the truths of the types and shadows of the Bible and particularly how the sacrifices associated with the old covenant involving God's ancient people Israel, symbolically spoke so much of the person and work of the Lord Jesus Christ who came to fulfil them all. It's no coincidence that the first declaration concerning the Lord Jesus, as He undertook His public ministry, identified Him as *the Lamb of God who takes away the sin of the world* (10).

The significance of that declaration to those who were so familiar with the necessary use of lambs in the sacrifices of the burnt offering, the sin offering and the Passover especially, would resonate deeply. So, as the Lord Himself invites us to remember Him - His life, His ministry, His death, His resurrection - in the bread and wine, so the typology of the old covenant sacrifices invites us to similarly consider the one who fulfils them, in the sacrifices of praise which follow, offered as expressions of thankful worship to His God and Father (11).

Our earlier verse in Heb.13:15 speaks both of 'sacrifice' and 'fruit'. We can readily link that with the Son of God who is appropriately the main focus of the substance, the content of our worship - the one who, as the grain of wheat, died in sacrificing Himself and in so doing has produced a great fruitful harvest (12). However, it's clear that these descriptors are to apply to the spiritual offerings that we bring to the Lord in collective worship. The reality of 'cost' is inextricably bound up in both these words. 'Fruit' is only forthcoming in any endeavour after a lot of patient and diligent work has been put in - a labour of love, often.

Likewise, such patient and diligent work invariably demands 'sacrifice' of some sort. As we think about the spiritual sacrifices that we would bring in worship to the Lord, we can learn a lot from the example of the psalmist who wrote,

My heart overflows with a good theme;

I address my verses to the King;

My tongue is the pen of a ready writer (13).

The 'verses' can also mean the 'workmanship' or 'composition' of the psalmist, which he addressed or presented to the King, who was also its subject and theme. There can be no greater theme, no greater subject for the substance of our worship offerings than the one who is the *"King of kings, and Lord of lords"* (14) and the one who is a *great King over all the earth* (15). It's good for us, then, to invest, as a labour of love and sacrifice, the necessary time in meditation in the Word of God. As we focus on the wonders of our God and on the loveliness of the Lord Jesus, the fruit that will inevitably come can be expressed from our hearts to our lips as an acceptable offering in worship to God who is worthy.

When such offerings consistently characterize the expressions of our appreciation of who the Lord is and what He has done, then not only is God glorified and honoured, but we will all come away from our time of remembrance with hearts warmed by our adoration of the one who first loved us! Surely the joy of collective worship delights the heart of God, but also enriches the offerer.

The principles of 'sacrifice' and 'fruit' apply equally to all the activities that we engage in collectively as a church and to the extent that these activities seek to honour and glorify the Lord, to proclaim His worth amongst ourselves or to others, they are expressions of worship. Our faithful and loving adherence to the many commands and exhortations that are embraced in the teaching of the Lord, and how they can be given expression in our collective service, provide many wonderful additional opportunities for us to continue to declare our heartfelt appreciation of who the Lord is.

References: (1) See NT Issue 1 2016 (2) Lk.22:19 (3) 1 Cor.11:23-26 (4) Matt.26:30; Mk.14:22-26 (5) 1 Cor.14:26 (6) Eph.5:19; Col.3:16 (7) 1 Cor.14:26,34 (8) 1 Pet.2:5b (9) 1 Pet.2:5a (10) Jn 1:29 (11) Rom.15:6 (12) Jn 12:24 (13) Ps.45:1 (14) Rev.19:16 (15) Ps.47:2

Bible quotations from the NASB.

3.4 COLLECTIVE PRAYER THAT POWERS (BRIAN JOHNSTON)

Why should we pray together as well as praying as individuals (aside from the fact we are commanded to)? Why have church prayer meetings? This chapter, based on the mention of the church prayers in Acts 2:41-42, is about collective prayer in church. It attempts to look at the advantage of communal prayer, fully accepting this seventh listed item in these verses is a characteristic function of a biblical church of God. We hope to establish that there's real power in praying together.

This becomes especially clear when we are brought together in crisis. Prayer is powerful when the congregation of God's people have a shared understanding of their need. This was the case when they approached Samuel at Mizpah in 1 Samuel 7. They were already aware of their need of God as they called on Samuel to lead them in intercessory prayer for God to deliver them from their enemies.

That occasion for prayer related to dealing with sin among God's people. We might pause to observe that the procedures God authorized for the forgiveness of sin among His people (1) showed a clear distinction between errors of the whole congregation (2) and those of individuals (3). The high priest represented the entire people in corporate approach to God (4). From such background material, we would wish to emphasize that corporate or church prayer is viewed differently by God from prayer even by groups of individuals. Turning now to the New Testament record, a look at a few examples of actual church of God prayer meetings serves to underscore the key point that they bring the corporate activities of the local church (and of the fellowship of the churches of God) to our attention.

In Acts 4:23-31 (ESV), we find the Church of God at Jerusalem in prayer. Prior to this, the apostles, Peter and John, had been arrested for performing a healing in the name of Jesus. It would appear their church friends had convened a church prayer gathering for...

> *When they were released, they went to their friends and reported what the chief priests and the elders had said to them. And when they heard it, they lifted their voices together to God and said, "Sovereign Lord, who made the heaven and the earth and the sea and everything in them, who through the mouth of our father David, your servant, said by the Holy Spirit, "'Why did the Gentiles rage, and the peoples plot in vain? The kings of the earth set themselves, and the rulers were gathered together, against the Lord and against his Anointed' - for truly in this city there were gathered together against your holy servant Jesus, whom you anointed, both Herod and Pontius Pilate, along with the Gentiles and the peoples of Israel, to do whatever your hand and your plan had predestined to take place.*
>
> *And now, Lord, look upon their threats and grant to your servants to continue to speak your word with all boldness, while you stretch out your hand to heal, and signs and wonders are performed through the name of your holy servant Jesus." And when they had prayed, the place in which they were gathered together was shaken, and they were all filled with the Holy Spirit and continued to speak the word of God with boldness.*

Peter and John surely felt supported in prayer. The church together brought its ongoing evangelical programme before God. It was not all about Peter and John. Through praying together about our shared activities we gain a sense of shared involvement in the life of the local church. This sense of mutual responsibility is largely developed in the prayer meeting. For it's there we face the strain of care together and express our emotional response to unfolding situations which affect us all as a believing community in our locality.

Has permission for a specific witness occasion been denied by the authorities? What if someone shares a strongly negative response they've received? We respond corporately by uniting in prayer for God's overruling. The challenges of recent missions to Zimbabwe and Mozambique energized prayer effectively across the international community that resulted in two churches being established. This is meaningful fellowship in the Gospel when in partnership together we engage in the furtherance of the 'Great Commission' (5).

In no other gathering of the church can the truth be better lived out that we are in character what the body of Christ is (6). In a well-functioning church prayer meeting, we lose sight of ourselves as individuals as we view ourselves in prayer as part of a whole. Whenever sincere and upright hearts are involved, this has the greatly beneficial effect of bringing us closer together, with a deepening sense of unity against a common foe. Nothing strengthens ties with each other and our respect for one another more than to hear each praying with integrity for the other (7). An example of this can be found in Acts 12:1-12:

> *Now about that time Herod the king laid hands on some who belonged to the church in order to mistreat them. And he had James the brother of John put to death with a sword. When he saw that it pleased the Jews, he proceeded to arrest Peter also ... On the very night when Herod was about to bring him forward ... an angel of the Lord suddenly appeared and ... struck Peter's side and woke him up ... his chains fell off his hands ... And he went out and continued to follow... they came to the iron gate that leads into the city, which opened for them by itself and they went out and went along one street, and immediately the angel departed from him ... And when he realized this, he went to the house of Mary, the mother of John who was also called Mark, where many were gathered together and were praying.*

I recollect a time when a life-threatening car accident had befallen a fellow-editor of Needed Truth magazine, Peter Hickling. Prayer was called for urgently across the worldwide community of churches of God. Those prayer gatherings were energised with a deep sense of dependence on God, as each prayer offered was aligned in agreement to ask for God's intervention. This displayed the efficacy of church prayers featuring a shared burden, intensively requested.

Such times show best our dependence on God, especially when it's a very focused, united, themed prayer meeting. It also demonstrates most clearly to us all how God listens. It reveals the power of prayer publicly. We are all witnesses of what we have asked for, and of that which we have received. A public prayer meeting is a witness to any observers as to how seriously we take the practice of the presence of God.

A Spirit-led church will be a prayer-led church, as we find in Acts 13:1-3:

> *Now there were at Antioch, in the church that was there, prophets and teachers: Barnabas, and Simeon who was called Niger, and Lucius of Cyrene, and Manaen who had been brought up with Herod the tetrarch, and Saul. While they were ministering to the Lord and fasting, the Holy Spirit said, "Set apart for Me Barnabas and Saul for the work to which I have called them." Then, when they had fasted and prayed and laid their hands on them, they sent them away.*

The church prayer meeting can become the source of initiative and of volunteers for the work of the Lord locally. It is such prayer times together in the presence of the Lord, and as led by his Spirit, that expand our vision of the Lord's work. It's then we 'lift up our eyes' to the sovereign Lord and then lift them up on the ripe harvest fields (8). God invites us to see things on a grander scale, and to broaden our horizons (9) beyond the confines of our own desires and at times rather petty ambitions. God's agenda is impressed on us for the advance of his kingdom and we are lifted out of our own little world. Of course, in the church prayer meeting, less mature believers learn the art of prayer. Different temperaments and styles can benefit greatly from interaction: the reserved and the effusive; the analytical and the emotional; the generalities and the specifics.

But what if the sense of power is lacking? How can we maximize the effectiveness of church prayer meetings on an 'average week'? In the opening chapter of this book, we were helpfully directed to the use of Scripture in prayer. A short additional ministry time before the church turns to prayer is helpful for focus. As we see from 2 Thessalonians 1:11 (NIV), the Apostle Paul did not turn to prayer with a blank mind, but after first bringing to mind relevant concerns. We do well to encourage informed praying at a church level (as well as personally), perhaps using a prayer-board to stimulate and collate prayer requests. Most importantly, brothers need to come with a real desire to lay hold of God. If the weekly programme allows, it may be better for the prayer gathering not to follow back-to-back after other church activities, so that saints can be fresh and focused before the Lord.

References: (1) Lev.4 (2) Lev.4:13 (3) Lev.4:27 (4) see Ex.28:29 (5) Matt.28:18-20 (6) 1 Cor.12:27 (7) Gal.6:2 (8) Jn 4:35 (9) Jn 14:12

Bible quotations from the NASB, unless otherwise stated.

PART 4: ABUNDANT WORSHIP

The fourth segment of the book is centred on worship, something that should be a central feature of our lives, as individuals and as part of a Church of God. In fact, it is no exaggeration to say that our worship is the central reason for our existence. That said, God intends for us to benefit greatly from the experience of worshipping Him. What do need to know about worship and how to worship?

In the first chapter, Stephen McCabe goes right back to basics and looks at the definition of worship and what it involves. In chapter two, James Needham focuses on the One whom we worship and reviews the examples of heavenly worship given us to in the New Testament book of Revelation.

The third chapter, from Dave Webster, views the subject through the lens of the individual and notes that for our worship to be truly meaningful it has to come at a personal cost to us – not a monetary cost, but a spiritual one. Finally, Richard Hutchinson bring this segment to a close with a look at a subject which does not perhaps receive the attention across Christendom that it truly deserves – God's purposes for a collective people to worship Him as God's (spiritual) House on earth today, just as He once had a (physical) House in Old Testament times. An appreciation of this great truth is bound to result in an abundance of worship!

4.1 WHAT IS WORSHIP? (STEPHEN MCCABE)

It has been said that we all worship something. We long to find something that gives our lives meaning; something that we can devote ourselves to. I read a recent research study that suggested that one of the surest ways to find satisfaction in life is to be part of something bigger than yourself that brings a sense of meaning and worth to your life. Of course, as Christians, we find ultimate worth in the person of God. Our word 'worship' is derived from the Old English 'weorþscipe', which meant 'to show honour' to something, likely to have developed from the thought of 'worthiness' or 'worth-ship'. At its simplest it is really about ascribing worth to God. What did the biblical writers mean?

There are several words that are translated as 'worship' in our Bible. Submission Hāwâ, or Shachah used in the Old Testament (OT), simply means 'to bow down' – a sign of acknowledging authority, and consequently showing honour and deference. This isn't used exclusively of God. For example, it is what the messenger did to David (1) when he reported the news of Saul and Jonathan's deaths. This word is echoed in the New Testament (NT) Greek proskyneō, which means 'to fall down and/or worship'. The Lord Jesus used this word when He said that the Father is seeking those who would worship Him in spirit and truth (2). The word indicates submission, and (something we will pick up on again) it is an external action that demonstrates an internal attitude.

Reverence

The Hebrew word emphasises the thought of a sense of awe inspired by our great God. In the Old Testament it is usually translated 'fear', 'revere', or 'worship', for example: *Now, Israel, what does the LORD your God require of you, but to fear the LORD your God, to walk in all His ways and love Him, and to serve the LORD your God with all your heart and with all your soul* (3). The New Testament word sebō simply means 'to worship' (for example, the Lord's condemnation of the vain worship of the Pharisees and scribes (4), but is also associated with the thought of fear or reverence in the narrative of Acts, where Gentiles associated themselves with synagogues and were seen as 'God-fearers' or 'worshippers of God' (5).

Service

Crucial to the biblical concept of worship isābad, which means 'to serve' – service and worship are very closely intertwined throughout Scripture because of the context of the service and worship of the house of God, which we can trace through both Old and New Testaments. God makes His appeal to Pharaoh through Moses: *Let My people go, that they may serve Me* (6) – service, or worship, made possible through the building of the tabernacle and the offerings brought to God there. Isaiah uses the word to speak of sacrificial worship (7).

Similarly, in the New Testament, the Greek latreuō refers to service (also translated worship) that is Godward in nature. Stephen uses it to speak of Israel coming out of Egypt to serve (worship) God (8) corresponding to the Hebrew ābad. From the biblical definitions given above, can we say what worship is not? It's not just thanksgiving. It's not just praise. Rather, it's about the stance of the heart towards God. That's what the Lord teaches us in Matthew 15 – worship is in vain if it is just words from the mouth (9). It must flow from an inward attitude; a continual posture of the heart.

Lives of Worship

Perhaps we can learn more by seeing lives of worship in action. The first time we read the word 'worship' in our Bibles is in Genesis 22: *Take now your son, your only son, whom you love ... and offer him ...* Abraham said to his young men, *Stay here ... I and the lad will go over there; and we will worship and return to you* (10). Worship in Genesis 22 is firmly in the context of costly sacrifice, absolute obedience, and heroic faith. Costly sacrifice because Abraham was willing to give the most precious thing in his life to God. Absolute obedience because he acted on that willingness without wavering, submitting to God's will.

God asked Abraham to give up his precious, promised child. Abraham's response was to get up early in the morning to do it! This is a life orientated toward God and His will. Heroic faith because, Hebrews says, even if Isaac had died that day (which was not God's purpose), Abraham believed that God was able to raise from the dead (11) in order to fulfil his promises to Abraham (12). Costly sacrifice, absolute obedience, and heroic faith will characterise a life of worship – a life centred on God. Another example is seen in Job. A poor servant runs to Job to share his devastating news: *Your sons and your daughters were eating and drinking wine in their oldest brother's house ... it fell on the young people and they died* (13). Job's telling response was to fall to the ground

It has been said that we all worship something. We long to find something that gives our lives meaning; something that we can devote ourselves to and worship. What was he doing? Job 1 demonstrates that his life was centred on God (14), and the perspective that gave him meant that he submitted to God in everything. He worshipped in good times and bad: *the LORD gave and the LORD has taken away. Blessed be the name of the Lord* (15). Job's life centred on God – he displayed a life of worship, despite the worst of circumstances.

Romans 12 gives us a New Testament, and present-day, view of what a life of worship really means. Paul encourages the believers in Rome to see that because of all the great truths of God's work of salvation (that Paul has been putting forward in his letter in preceding chapters), they should be presenting their bodies, their whole beings, as a living, ongoing, committed, sacrifice to God (16) What does it mean in practice? Lives centred on God, so that we are completely devoted to Him, and all those practical acts of goodness that Paul then details (17), flow from our living sacrifice to God – our service of worship to Him.

Our living sacrifice is to be acceptable to God, or well-pleasing to Him. That means it should be holy, just as He is holy; set apart for Him and His use and pleasure. Paul says that this is your spiritual service of worship. Some translations say "your rational service of worship". Serving and worshipping God are intertwined; the focus of a life that isn't being conformed to this present world, but is instead being transformed through a mind continually centred on God and His things (18). This giving our bodies over to serving God each day is worship, and is the logical, rational, response to what God has done for us. An ongoing stance of worship in our lives expresses the internal attitude that God is the centre of all things and I must fit my life around Him, rather than demanding that He fit into my life.

Self-centredness or God-centredness?

And so we come to an obstacle that can get in the way of a life of worship – self-centredness. It's the antithesis of a life centred on God – of a heart that submits to, reverences, and serves God through sacrificial giving.

Sometimes we may place ourselves at the centre of our own world, demanding that others revolve around us. However, if we understand that God is the centre of everything (from Him and through Him and to Him are all things. To Him be the glory forever (19), then He must also be at the centre of our little lives. It is we who must fit in around Him and His purposes. That's a life of worship. When we look at the Godhead, we find that the Son, even with His suffering looming, was seeking the glory of His Father (20). We find that the Father purposes to glorify the Son (21). We find that the Spirit seeks to glorify the Son by disclosing the things of God to us through the Scriptures (22) – that brings glory to the Son, who brings glory to the Father.

This God-centredness, so to speak, is what we are invited into in a life of worship. We have the opportunity, through God's transforming of our lives, to stop demanding that people revolve around us and rather to centre our lives on God, letting Him be the weightiest consideration in our lives as we seek to present ourselves as living sacrifices – our spiritual service of worship. William Temple rightly said, 'Worship is the submission of all our nature to God. It is the quickening of the conscience by His holiness; the nourishment of mind with His truth; the purifying of imagination by His beauty; the opening of the heart to His love; the surrender of will to His purpose—all this gathered up in adoration, the most selfless emotion of which our nature is capable' (23).

Worship, ascribing to Him worth, is really our ultimate response to God. It is not simply an external act (though our corporate worship as the people of God is surely the highest of expressions of worship), but is a continual posture of heart towards our Creator and Redeemer; a way of life that places Him at the centre, and from which praise, thankfulness, sacrifice and obedience flow.

References: (1) 2 Sam.1:2 (2) Jn 4:21-24 (3) Deut.10:12 (4) Matt.15:1,9; Mk.7:7 (5) Acts 13:43;16:14 (6) Ex.8:1 (7) Isa.19:21 (8) Acts 7:7 (9) Matt.15:7-9 (10) Gen.22:1-5 (11) Heb.11:17-19 (12) Gen.12:1-3; 15:4-5 (13) Job 1:18-19 (14) See Job 1:1,5,8 (15) Job 1:21 (16) Rom.12:1-2 (17) Rom.12:9-21 (18) Col.3:2; Phil.4:8 (19) Rom.11:36 (20) Jn 17:1 (21) Jn 13:31-32;17:5; Heb.1:5-13 (22) Jn 16:14 (23) Wm. Temple, Readings in St John's Gospel, Macmillan 1945.

Bible quotations from the NASB.

4.2 WORSHIPPING GOD (JAMES NEEDHAM)

When God fills the hands of His servants with a work to be done for Him, we can be sure He takes care to prepare them for the task. The greater the burden, the greater the preparation must be, and it was surely a heavy burden that lay in store for John as he heard the Lord declare *I will show you what must take place after this* (1). The record of the Revelation is startling to us who read it; but to John it was more immediate, more terrible still, as he saw unfold before his eyes the predestined course for this corrupted world. What could prepare the old apostle for such a vision? Only this: the realisation that, through it all, God was on the throne. Though despised and refused on earth, He was worshipped and adored in heaven, and, possessing absolute authority, in full control of it all.

The majesty of God Revelation 4 and 5 reveal the marvellous beauty of the scene presented to John as he passed through the door standing open in heaven. Before him stood a throne, and upon it one who had the appearance of jasper and carnelian, whose splendour cast an emerald rainbow in the brightness of heaven. Ezekiel, in his preparation, had seen the same throne as he stood by the banks of the Chebar and gazed upon one whose appearance was *as it were gleaming metal … as it were the appearance of fire, and there was brightness around him* (2). Jasper and carnelian are gemstones bearing the colours of fire and capable of the highest polish. These stones describe His glory, just as John would later see the new Jerusalem coming down out of heaven having the glory of God, its radiance like a most rare jewel, like a jasper, clear as crystal (3).

Searching for ways to describe what he saw, John gazed upon the glory of God, burning in holiness and casting a brightness so intense that it created a rainbow in heaven. Since the days of Noah, the rainbow had been a reminder of God's covenant never again to judge mankind by a flood (4). On earth it would appear for a time, as sunlight shone through the darkness of the rainclouds, and then it would vanish. Not so in heaven, as Ezekiel and John traced its presence to the throne, where it remained an eternal reminder of the steadfast grace of God, sending a glorious shaft of light through all the darkness of sin which had enveloped creation.

The Worship of Heaven

Around this majestic display of the beauty and authority of God were four living creatures, full of eyes in front and behind (5). Writing to the Ephesians, Paul expressed his wish that God might give them a spirit of wisdom and of revelation in the knowledge of him, having the eyes of your hearts enlightened (6). Adorned with many eyes, and so enlightened in the revelation of their knowledge of God, their worship was ceaseless: *Holy, holy, holy, is the Lord God Almighty, who was and is and is to come!* (5). The worship of the angels began with who God is. His holiness, His power and His eternity are intrinsic characteristics of the nature of God and they inspire the worship of heaven, for at the sound of that refrain twenty-four elders fell from their thrones.

We may speculate whether the twenty-four elders are themselves an order of angelic beings, or redeemed ones now gathered to glory. The purity of their garments, the honour of their crowns and the authority of their thrones all suggest that these had been faithful overcomers in mortal life (7), but now they cast before God all that was honourable to them. God had given them their crowns, but how could they wear them in the presence of Him to whom all glory and honour and power belongs? So, in worship, they glorified God and abased themselves, abandoning all the symbols of their worthiness to Him who alone is worthy!

Their song to Him was the song of old, which had filled heaven when earth's foundations were laid *when the morning stars sang together and all the sons of God shouted for joy* (8): *you created all things, and by your will they existed and were created* (9). As the scene moves into chapter 5, the worship of heaven becomes occupied with 'the Lamb' who stands in the midst as one freshly slain. Before Him, the living creatures and the twenty-four elders fall, the old song of creation giving way to the new song of redemption (10). Its subject is the Lamb who, by His death, *has ransomed people for God from every tribe and language and people and nation* (11), and in its melody thousands of thousands join; every creature united in the chorus proclaiming the worth of the Lamb.

The first chapter in this series traced the connection between worth and worship. It is a connection found in heaven's praises, where both God and the Lamb are declared to be worthy. In the original language, the word is axios and carries the thought of being weighed out and found equal to something corresponding in value. Outside of Revelation 4 and 5, axios is used in a material context to describe the worthiness of a labourer to receive his wages (12) and in a spiritual context to describe the unworthiness of man before God (13). Only within these chapters is axios used about God, for in heaven the measure is altogether different. Before the presence of the majesty of God, there is no creature who is found worthy (14), for none but the Lamb can equal the weight of the value of God. There, their worth is unequalled and unchallenged.

The Lamb once crucified beside a thief who acknowledged the weight of his deeds in his worthiness of death (15), is now acknowledged by myriads as worthy of the full weight of their adoration.

The Worship of a People

In Hebrews 12, having reached the climax of his letter in the access given to the people of God to enter through the veil and worship in God's presence above (16), the writer compares that present experience with the experience of Israel in their flight from Egypt. Then, released from bondage to service (17), they came to Sinai to receive the covenant and instructions for worship. Today, the people of God have also come to a mountain, but one which does not rise from the wilderness floor, and at whose summit stands the heavenly Jerusalem. The old order – the encampment of Israel and the tents of the Levites – are replaced by innumerable angels in festal gathering ... the assembly of the firstborn who are enrolled in heaven (18). And so a redeemed and gathered-together people, purchased by blood to be *a kingdom and priests to our God* (19), enter in to appear before God in the presence of the hosts of heaven.

The God who sits enthroned in heaven is worthy of our adoration. His holiness, might and eternity, which form the constant refrain of those gathered around His throne, should fill our minds too until, taken up with His person, our worship overflows with rejoicing at His gracious design fulfilled in Christ. Today, God is seeking worshippers whose heartfelt response reflects the elders in heaven, who, measuring their worth against the worth of God, count themselves nothing and fall before His throne, casting to Him their every honour, and offering up from filled hands and redeemed hearts the full weight of their adoring worship.

There within the veil, as a people ascends to worship, His delight and ours shall be one, for He and we will be taken up with the wonder and beauty of the Son, of whom God never tires to hear. And our voices shall mingle with the heavenly throng in the new song of redemption which echoes around the throne: *Worthy is the Lamb who was slain!* (20).

> Though fails our understanding dull
>
> His worth to compass to the full,
>
> We yet would speak of Him to Thee;
>
> Dear to Thyself and us is He. (21)

References: (1) Rev.4:1 (2) Ezek.1:27 (3) Rev.21:11 (4) Gen.9:13-15 (5) Rev.4:6 (6) Eph.1:17-18 (7) Rev.2:10, 26-27; 3:4-5 (8) Job 38:7 (9) Rev.4:11 (10) Rev.5:8-10; Ps.40:2-3; 96:1-2 (11) Rev.5:9 (12) Matt.10:10 (13) Jn 1:27 (14) Rev.5:4 (15) Lk.23:41 (16) Heb.10:19-20 (17) Ex.5:1; 8:1 (18) Heb.12:22-23 (19) Rev.5:10 (20) Rev.5:12 (21) C. Belton, PHSS, 110

Bible quotations from the ESV.

4.3 INDIVIDUAL WORSHIP AND SACRIFICE (DAVE WEBSTER)

We have already learned that to worship is to show honour to something or to express worthiness or 'worthship' to something or someone. 'At its simplest it is really ascribing worth to God' (1). Some people think of going to church as worship and, using 'church' in its common use like this, there is a lot of truth in that. But, of course, the Bible teaches that 'church' is people (2). So it is more accurate to think of the church coming together to worship. But what about when the time of being together is over, or has not yet come?

I Should Praise God

Who cannot be moved by the thought that God does not treat us as our sins deserve or repay us according to our iniquities? (3) He is a Father showing compassion and yet He is King of everything! He is very great and clothed with splendour and majesty (4). He is the creator and He keeps creation under control, providing good things to human beings and the animals. We are moved to worship the God to whom we can say: How many are your works, LORD! In wisdom you made them all; the earth is full of your creatures (5). And we learn that worship is a life-long response to such a God: *I will sing to the LORD all my life; I will sing praise to my God as long as I live. May my meditation be pleasing to him, as I rejoice in the LORD* (6).

I can't praise and moan at the same time! Moaning is feeling sorry for myself and imagining that everything has gone wrong! The Christian writer J. John put it like this: 'Give time to praising God, as a response to all he has done. This is one of the best antidotes to this generation's biggest problem, which is our obsession with ourselves. When we turn to God and put him at the centre of our lives, we take the focus off ourselves and put it on to him. Focus on him – worshipping and thanking him for all he has done' (7).

I Should Be Thankful

It is a good idea to think of things that are a blessing in our lives and to specifically thank God for them in a spirit of worship. *And whatever you do, whether in word or deed, do it all in the name of the Lord Jesus, giving thanks to God the Father through him* (8). That includes my times of worship and prayer. Think about God. He is good! He has created a marvellous world. He has redeemed me and saved me! Think about the Lord Jesus on that awful cross. God delivers me from danger and cares for me. He is so patient with me! It is good to remind ourselves in God's presence that *Every good and perfect gift is from above, coming down from the Father of the heavenly lights, who does not change like shifting shadows* (9).

I Can't Worship Without Cost

Let's not pretend that following the Lord and bringing worship and praise through holy, obedient lives will be an easy thing! The Lord Jesus spoke about the broad road that leads to destruction (10) – the way everyone else seems to be going. If you and I want an easy life we should just follow the crowd. Instead we are called to unconditional following – that includes giving up things that we would naturally enjoy (11)! Think about Abraham. The first time worship is mentioned in the Bible is when Abraham was instructed by God to *take your son, your only son, whom you love – Isaac – and go to the region of Moriah. Sacrifice him there as a burnt offering on a mountain I will show you* (12). Abraham's reply to his servants was: *Stay here with the donkey while I and the boy go over there. We will worship and then we will come back to you* (13).

Worship, for Abraham, was being prepared to give up his dearest possession while still acknowledging God's right to ask for it and while still believing in the promises God had made concerning Isaac. King David, under very different circumstances, understood the cost involved in worship and sacrifice to his God. David was instructed to build an altar to the Lord on Araunah's threshing floor. Araunah was prepared to let David have it as a gift: *But the king replied* to Araunah, *"No, I insist on paying you for it. I will not sacrifice to the LORD my God burnt offerings that cost me nothing."* So David bought the threshing floor and the oxen and paid fifty shekels of silver for them (14).

Any life choices that are offered as a sacrifice of worship to our God will have to cost us something. It may cost you a friendship. It may cost you a promotion. It may be doing without something so that you can contribute money to the work of the Lord. It may be just turning the TV off! It will certainly cost you time and effort. We need to set aside time to think about what God has done for us and worship Him for all He is and does for us.

I Must Worship

We should stop thinking of worship as a chore to be done! Instead, we should regard it as the normal response to our God who is absolutely worthy of praise. We can then see how it fits in to our everyday spiritual lives. C.S. Lewis suggests that it helps to ask what we mean when we say that a picture or work of art is 'admirable' or to be praised. It is not because it will lose out if we don't praise it but, he argues, that '... admiration is the correct, adequate, appropriate, response to it, that if paid, admiration will not be "thrown away", and that if we do not admire we shall be stupid, insensible, and great losers, we shall have missed something' (15). That's exactly the point. If I don't worship God I lose out! God's glory is not in the least diminished. I must worship the God who is there, who is in control and who loves me so much. As true worshippers we find delight in our God and His Word, we gaze on the beauty of the LORD (16) and we appreciate something of the glory of our God (17).

I Should Worship Every Day

Worship is not to be confined to those times in our lives that are especially devoted to God: our gathering together as a church, our morning devotionals or our preparations for collective worship. Rather it is all-encompassing. Having spent most of his letter to the Romans explaining the theology of salvation and the Gospel, Paul writes: *Therefore, I urge you, brothers, in view of God's mercy, to offer your bodies as living sacrifices, holy and pleasing to God – this is your spiritual act of worship* (18).

I am to offer myself to God as an act of worship and service. That means my day, my time and energy, my relationships, my thoughts, my attitudes, what I do and where I go – all are to be given to God. As I 'worship' they can be offered, sacrificially, to the God who has done so much for me in sending the Lord Jesus Christ to be my Saviour and Redeemer. Not just my 'Quiet Time' but also my 'Me Time'! But it's so good to get to this point. Just as the picturesque view is worth the long, hard walk and seeing the happy faces of the youth club children is worth the rush from work, so the glimpse of God I get from my worship (the continual offering of myself to God) and daily activities is worth whatever has been given up or re-arranged to get there. Are we prepared to make time to worship God as individual Christians? That's the very real challenge of living worshipful Christian lives in today's society.

References: (1) Stephen McCabe, NT 2016 'What is Worship?' (2) See, for example, 1 Cor.11:18 (3) Ps.103:10 (4) Ps.104:1 (5) Ps.104:24 (6) Ps.104:33-34 (7) J John, Ten, Kingsway Publications (8) Col.3:17 (9) Jas.1:17 (10) Matt.7:13 (11) See Matt.16:24 (12) Gen.22:2 (13) Gen.22:5 (14) 2 Sam.24:24 (15) C.S. Lewis, Reflections on the Psalms, Chapter 9, Collins (16) Ps.27:4 (17) See Ps.8:1; 19:1 (18) Rom.12:1 (NIV 1984 edition)

Bible quotations from the NIV, unless otherwise stated.

4.4 THE COLLECTIVE WORSHIP OF THE PEOPLE OF GOD (RICHARD HUTCHINSON)

Imagine how it must have felt for the people who had travelled from the far reaches of the kingdom, a journey of many days, to finally see Jerusalem on the heights of Zion, the streams of their fellow Israelites flowing upwards to the place of worship (1) with the strains of the Psalms of Ascents drifting through the crowds: *Let us go to his dwelling place. Let us worship at his footstool!* (2) *Behold, how good and pleasant it is when brothers dwell in unity!* (3) *Come, bless the LORD, all you servants of the LORD ... Lift up your hands to the holy place and bless the LORD* (4). It must have thrilled the heart of God to watch that joyous procession.

When God first called Abram to leave the land of the Chaldeans, He was looking forward to the people He would create through that man of faith entering into a covenant relationship *to be God to you and to your offspring after you* (5). The promise of possessing the land came with the same provision: *I will be their God* (6), and later God spoke of those *whom I brought out of the land of Egypt in the sight of the nations, that I might be their God* (7). Repeatedly, throughout the Old Testament, as His people's faithfulness routinely dissolved into idolatry, God spoke the same words to them by His prophets, that if they would only return to Him then *they shall be my people, and I will be their God* (8).

It is so consistent a theme of Scripture that we cannot help but see it as a central desire of the heart of God to have a people who were united in their recognition of who He is. "I will be their God" was a commitment to that people. Physically, He would be a protector and provider for them, and spiritually, the one who would establish the shalom (9) of His people, that state of absolute well-being, the blessedness of God. The second part of that dynamic was that Israel would be His people. Their role was to honour and serve obediently. God told

Pharaoh to let His people go *that they may serve me* (10). This was not physically, as they had served Pharaoh, but in worship, which, as we've seen earlier in this series, was intrinsic to their service (11).

The obedience required was not merely a condition of God's blessing but, more properly, their worshipful obedience was the vehicle of God's blessing. The experience of blessedness, of shalom, was only to be found in a life oriented by the reality of a holy God, as revealed in His law (12). The spiritual purpose of that code of statutes and commandments was to instruct their hearts in the nature of God's character, which is why it so captivated the heart of a man like David. The practical purpose of the Law was to preserve their sanctity as God's holy people, maintaining their fitness to worship together the God it taught them to adore.

God had declared that they would be a kingdom of priests (13) and His intention was for this to be a people characterized by their worship, by the intimacy of their connection to the God they served. He dwelt amongst them, sanctifying the people by His presence (14), and He made it clear to them that they were to come together to worship in the place of His choosing, where He set His name (15). There was one place particularly specified to prevent everyone from doing their own thing and worshipping as they saw fit (16). God wanted His people to come to a specific place, with specific sacrifices in accordance with His plan for His people.

God's heart has not changed. It is still His desire to have a united people who join together in the place He has chosen and upon which He has placed His name, to offer up their worship to Him as a kingdom of priests. He still wants to be their God and for them to be His people, and He has made His dwelling among them to sanctify them by His presence (17). We, today, will still find shalom to the degree to which we orient our individual lives worshipfully towards God, but God asks for more than individual honour. He made us a people for His praise, a nation by faith, formed under a new covenant but with the same purpose – to be characterized by our worship and service to the God we adore (18).

God still richly values the collective worship of His people, and so should we. We have been called into fellowship with each other, as well as fellowship with the Father, Son and Spirit, because the Lord wants us to experience the joy of worshipping together, of building relationships around the shared faith, communal joy and mutual hope we hold together. Our collective worship is greater than the sum of its parts, as we blend our individual appreciation and perspective into a congregated offering that is expressed on behalf of all and confirmed by all through the Amen we raise together.

The experience of the people of Israel, wending their way towards Jerusalem at set times in the year for festival worship, has been eclipsed by the provision God has made for the people He has created through Christ Jesus. God has called us to worship collectively on the first day of every week, coming together from all across the earth, meeting locally in our own buildings but, spiritually, ascending by faith to the heights of heaven itself (19). There we do not approach the altar of sacrifice to present our offering to the priests, but our Great High Priest brings us into the very presence of God, the Holy Place (20), where we worship intimately, offering our thanksgivings for the once-for-all sacrifice of His Son that has secured our eternal salvation and established our inheritance with Him.

It requires faith to look at our Breaking of the Bread remembrance services and see past the very human elements – our faltering (or overly verbose) thanksgivings, our sometimes ropey or weak singing, the noise of the world going on around us – and recognize that something intensely spiritual is happening. The writer to the Hebrews paints a vivid picture of where we truly ascend to:

> *But you have come to Mount Zion and to the city of the living God, the heavenly Jerusalem, and to innumerable angels in festal gathering, and to the assembly of the firstborn who are enrolled in heaven, and to God, the judge of all, and to the spirits of the righteous made perfect, and to Jesus, the mediator of a new covenant, and to the sprinkled blood that speaks a better word than the blood of Abel* (21).

We gather locally, across the globe, but we are found in heaven itself and we worship in the company of angels, before the very throne of Almighty God, with our precious High Priest present, without whom we simply could not contemplate standing in that place. As someone who is part of a remote church of God, it is a very special truth to my heart that the small group I meet with in a Jewish community centre in Vancouver is, in truth, worshipping in the sanctity of the heavenly temple, together with saints in Cullybackey, in Lumbadze, in Melbourne, in Rajahmundry ... each and every church of God in the Fellowship meeting locally, but coming together to the one appointed place as the worshipping people of God to give Him the honour of which He is worthy. In this way we are accomplishing for God that great desire of His heart.

We are His treasured possession, a people functioning together as a holy priesthood and proclaiming His glory. We are not yet the perfect expression of that desire, but how moving it is to read, in the final chapters of Scripture, John's description of the new Jerusalem descending from heaven to the new earth with that proclamation ringing out once more, this time for eternity: I heard a loud voice from the throne saying, *Behold, the dwelling place of God is with man. He will dwell with them, and they will be his people, and God himself will be with them as their God* (22). Then the heart of God will be wholly satisfied and we, His people, including then the whole of the Church the Body of Christ, will know complete Shalom in our eternal worship together.

References: (1) Jer.31:12, RV (2) Ps.132:7 (3) Ps.133:1 (4) Ps.134:1-2 (5) Gen.17:7 (6) Gen.17:8 (7) Lev.26:45 (8) some examples include: Jer.24:7; Ezek.11:20; Zech.8:8 (9) Strong's Concordance, Gk. Shalom, meaning completeness, soundness, welfare, peace. See Num.6:26; 25:12 (10) Ex.7:16 (11) cf. Stephen McCabe, NT 2016, 'What is Worship?' (12) Ps.112:1 (13) Ex.19:6 (14) Ex.29:43-45 (15) Deut.12:5-6 and (16) Deut.12:8 (17) 2 Cor.6:16 (18) 1 Pet.2:5 (19) Heb.9:24 (20) Heb.10:19-22 (21) Heb.12:22-24; see also 9:24 & 10:19 (22) Rev.21:3

Bible quotations from the ESV, unless otherwise stated.

PART 5: ABUNDANT GIVING

The fifth segment of this book is al about our giving. Edwin Neely starts off with an overview of giving to God, recognizing that while we all have the ability to give (regardless of our financial situation), our attitude and approach is vital, because we are accountable to God as stewards of the resources He has given to us.

Gareth Andrews drills down into one particular aspect of our giving in chapter 2 – our giving to others using the wonderful example of the Macedonia church in the New Testament as a blueprint. Andy Seddon explores another important aspect in the third chapter, which is giving God-ward. Even though God does not need our money, when we give it willingly in His service it is very precious to Him, particularly as it relates to the maintenance of His House.

Finally, Lennie Shaw reminds us that God loves a cheerful giver, and we shouldn't begrudge giving to others and to God – after all, that just will rob us of the abundant joy that God intends for us to experience!

5.1 GIVING TO GOD (EDWIN NEELY)

In Genesis 43 Jacob suggested that his sons go back to Egypt for food and with them take a present to the lord of the land. Had he realized just who the lord was, what the eventual outcome would be, all that was involved in giving, would he have suggested a little balm, a little honey, a little anything? Would he not have given all that he had, himself included? (1) We are given the tremendous opportunity to give to the Lord of heaven, the one for whom, through whom and to whom are all things. Are we still fixated on a little?

Of those noble saints in Macedonia Paul records: they first gave themselves to the Lord (2). That is where giving to God must begin. Giving will not make a Christian more spiritual. Spirituality, however, may well lead to giving. And where spirituality is lacking, God has no use for conscience money, money given to make up for spiritual shortcomings. God does not need our money (3). The earth is the Lord's and all it contains (4). He gives us the opportunity to give so that He might abundantly bless us with more, both here and hereafter (5): *Give, and it will be given to you ... good measure—pressed down, shaken together, and running over. For by your standard of measure it will be measured to you in return* (6).

The Bible gives some very practical guidelines about giving to God. Here are a few:

Ability

Poverty is not an excuse not to give. Again the Macedonian churches are cited as examples: *... their deep poverty overflowed in the wealth of their liberality* (7). And the poor widow who gave so generously to the treasury as the Lord looked on, stands out as a shining example to us all (8). The Lord still watches the treasury! Nevertheless, Scripture also teaches balance in the matter. A person should not go into debt in order to give to God. Paul teaches clearly that ... *it is acceptable according to what a person has, not according to what he does not have*

(9). He also makes clear that giving is to be as a person may prosper (10). But we are often amazed how prosperity follows that initial giving. God remains debtor to no one.

Attitude

Another of the guidelines discusses our attitude in giving. God loves a cheerful giver (11). This goes along with the willing spirit that God so desires. In the Old Testament Israel met the standard: *Then the people rejoiced because they had offered so willingly, for they made their offering to the LORD with a whole heart, and King David also rejoiced greatly* (12). 1 Chronicles 29 has several pertinent things to say about the subject at hand. Verse 12: *Both riches and honour come from You ... and it lies in Your hand to make great and to strengthen everyone.* Verse 14: *Who am I and who are my people that we should be able to offer as generously as this? For all things come from You, and from Your hand we have given You.*

God gives; we are blessed; and then we are doubly blessed in giving. In the New Testament, Paul rejoiced when individuals and churches rose to their God-given responsibilities (13). And in both Old and New Testaments God was well-pleased. God also leaves instruction that privacy should be a motivating factor in our generosity: *Beware of practising your righteousness before men to be noticed by them; otherwise you have no reward with your Father who is in heaven.* The Lord Jesus then spoke on and in the next few verses Matthew records for us just how that is to affect our giving. Notice that the Lord does not say, 'if' you give in these verses, but 'when' you give, and He uses the often quoted phrase *"do not let your left hand know what your right hand is doing"* and finishes by stating ... *your giving will be in secret; and your Father who sees what is done in secret will reward you* (14).

Tied in with this is also the subject of humility in giving. When Israel offered their first fruits the offerers came in remembrance of where they had originated, the hole of the pit from whence they had been extricated, expressed their thankfulness at the beneficence of God, and in worship presented their physical bounty and their spiritual sacrifices as well, rejoicing in their God-given ability to give (15). Notice that what they were commanded to bring was the tithe, ten per cent of their prosperity. While we are not so bound in this day of grace, that commandment was never rescinded. Our joy should be that we are not limited to the tithe, and any restrictions of income tax laws and benefits should not enter the equation at all.

Approach

Another matter that this portion brings to our attention is that giving to God should be of the first fruits of His bounty to us, not the leftovers when all else has been cared for. A brilliant example of God's way of doing things is seen in 1 Kings 17:7-14. A widow with little to give and in great distress is asked first to supply to God's prophet, Elisha, the last morsel that she possessed. Her faithfulness in doing so was rewarded by God, her jar of oil and bowl of flour not failing until the famine that plagued the land had subsided. *Honor the LORD from your wealth and from the first of all your produce; so your barns will be filled with plenty and your vats will overflow with new wine* (16).

It is probably true in your case, as in mine, that there are those in our churches with deeper pockets and bigger hearts than we have, and perhaps seemingly fewer fiscal problems. That should in no way influence the subject of our giving. We are not called upon to sit back and let others do what is necessary. We are to do our part, however that compares with what others may give. *Now this I say*, writes Paul, *he who sows sparingly will also reap sparingly, and he who sows bountifully will also reap bountifully* (17). The God who knows all about bountiful giving also knows all about bountiful rewarding.

As in our secular handling of finance, we will probably find that systematic giving is helpful in keeping us on track. Paul instructed the Corinthians to weekly set aside their givings, saving them for the appropriate time, as the Lord prospered them (18). Some orderly method of giving might also assist us in our striving to please the One who gave so freely for us. Some practical lessons might be taken from the financial business world. The use of credit cards and bank debit cards has mushroomed in recent years, so that in some areas there is practically a cashless society. The fact is when we use a credit card we are for the moment spending someone else's money, and somehow we have less difficulty doing that than spending our own. We need to ask ourselves whose money we are handling anyway.

Accountability

We get used to thinking of my pay cheque, my pocket money, my bank account, when we should realize that whatever possessions that we handle are only in our hands because they have been placed under our stewardship. *What do you have that you did not receive?* asks Paul *And if you did receive it, why do you boast as if you had not received it* (19)? Moses said, *Otherwise, you may say in your heart, 'My power and the strength of my hand made me this wealth'. But you shall remember the LORD your God, for it is He who is giving you power to make wealth* (20). It is true that control of that wealth is in our hands meantime, but so is the responsibility to disperse it to the glory of God (21)

The talent hidden in the handkerchief receives no reward; indeed, the mishandling of the Lord's money brings judgment (22). Paul points out that anything done without love as the motivator is valueless in the sight of God (23). Someone has also added that it is possible to give without love, but it is impossible to love without giving. Pursue love! (24) Both Matthew and Luke quoted Christ: *... you cannot serve God and wealth* (25). But we can serve God with our money. The Lord also said, *It is more blessed to give than to receive* (26).

The sheer number of scriptures on this subject of giving should waken us to greater responsibility! Herbert Lockyer tells the story of the prosperous farmer who was questioned by his neighbours about how he could give so freely, yet always have more to give. His response was that the answer was easy. "I keep shovelling into God's barn and He keeps shovelling into mine. He has the bigger shovel!"

References: (1) Gen.46:1 (2) 2 Cor.8:5 (3) Ps.50:12 (4) Ps.24:1 (5) Mal.3:10 (6) Lk.6:38 (7) 2 Cor.8:2 (8) Mk.12:43-44 (9) 2 Cor.8:12 (10) 1 Cor.16:2 (11) 2 Cor.9:7 (12) 1 Chron.29:9 (13) 2 Cor.8:2; Phil.4:16-18 (14) Matt.6:1-4

(15) Deut.26:1-17 (16) Prov.3:9-10 (17) 2 Cor.9:6 (18) 1 Cor.16:1-2 (19) 1 Cor.4:7 (20) Deut.8:17-18 (21) Acts 5:4 (22) Lk.19:20,26 (23) 1 Cor.13:1-3 (24) 1 Cor.14:1 (25) Matt.6:24; Lk.16:13 (26) Acts 20:35

Bible quotations from the NASB.

5.2 GIVING TO SUPPORT OTHERS (GARETH ANDREWS)

In our first chapter on giving, we started to consider the example of the saints in Macedonia, recorded for us by Paul in 2 Corinthians 8 and 9. Here Paul wanted to share their wonderful example with the brothers and sisters in Corinth, and specifically their act of grace (1) in giving to support others in the Church of God in Jerusalem. It is the specific circumstances of this generosity that are still truly remarkable, and maybe even counter-intuitive to us, as we read about it today.

In the midst of a very severe trial, their overflowing joy and their extreme poverty welled up in rich generosity (2). Where, then, did this joyful conviction and selfless impulse come from? Naturally speaking, it is often when things are going well for us, when we're happy and content and feel that we have enough for our own needs, that we might then start to feel more generous and comfortable to share the rest with others. But that was not a situation in which these dear Christians found themselves. They were being severely tested, but they were filled with abundant joy. They knew extreme poverty, but were overflowing with a wealth of generosity; not just according to their means, but even beyond their means, begging us earnestly for the favor of taking part in the relief of the saints (3).

What a contrast with our natural selfish tendencies, and what an example to the church in Corinth then – and to us today! It has been suggested that our problem in society today is not that people do not know that they should support and help the poor, but rather people do know and yet are not truly motivated to do so in their hearts. We live in a time of staggering inequality. It has recently been reported by the charity Oxfam that the 62 richest individuals in the world now own the same wealth as the poorest 3,600,000,000 combined (that is, half the world's population!). We also live in a materialistic age where neither legislation, nor knowledge, nor appeals to morals, reason or even love can slow, much less stop, the divide from increasing between rich and poor.

So in the midst of this age, what greater motivation is there for us to give than the experience, appreciation and joyful awe of God's grace in our redemption, and a growing respect and love for others as we appreciate their value in God's estimation. The act of grace of the saints in Macedonia was made possible because of the gift of the grace of God that had been given to them (4). In other words, they were able and motivated to show rich kindness to others because they had first received and experienced the greater unmerited favour of God in redemption: *For you know the grace of our Lord Jesus Christ, that though he was rich, yet for your sake he became poor, so that you by his poverty might become rich* (5).

What a supreme example we see, then, in the divine selflessness and generosity of God, unparalleled and unbounded: *For from his fullness we have all received, grace upon grace* (6). In comparison to the fullness of the spiritual riches we have received through His poverty, any material poverty that we might have to face is ultimately fleeting and inconsequential. So the gift of grace to us should always lead us to acts of grace to support others. That was certainly the experience of the first Christians (7). We read of how the believers in Jerusalem had glad and generous hearts, and isn't that strikingly similar to the abundance of joy and the overflowing wealth of generosity that was demonstrated by the Macedonians?

God loves a cheerful giver (8) and it was not a commandment or an imposed legal or socialistic framework that led to their selling possessions and giving to those in need. Rather, it was their joy and their unity in heart and mind that meant there was not a needy person among them (9). Here, in God's grace, we see selflessness and love in action within a community and fellowship of equals. Surely this was – and is – a better basis of mutual support and equality than any of the flawed extremes and failures of humanly devised social frameworks: more driven than capitalism, more equitable than communism.

In the mistakes of Ananias and Sapphira (misleading and lying) within this same community in Acts 5, we are reminded of the continuing tension between our own natural tendency to desire self-sufficiency, by holding back for ourselves, compared to the voluntary act of grace and faith in giving to support others while totally relying on God. Looking at the Old Testament, the scholar Bruce Waltke concluded: 'The wicked advantage themselves by disadvantaging others, but the righteous disadvantage themselves to advantage others' (10). Today, are you or I truly willing to disadvantage ourselves to advance the community? What will that mean in practice from week to week? Surely we can start by seeing giving as an opportunity and a privilege as opposed to an obligation or a burden and that itself should be an indicator of our spiritual maturity. James says:

> *What good is it, my brothers, if someone says he has faith but does not have works? Can that faith save him? If a brother or sister is poorly clothed and lacking in daily food, and one of you says to them, "Go in peace, be warmed and filled," without giving them the things needed for the body, what good is that? So also faith by itself, if it does not have works, is dead* (11).

When giving the law, Moses told the children of Israel to change their hearts:

> *... be no longer stubborn. For the LORD your God is God of gods and Lord of lords, the great, the mighty, and the awesome God, who is not partial and takes no bribe. He executes justice for the fatherless and the widow, and loves the sojourner, giving him food and clothing. Love the sojourner, therefore, for you were sojourners in the land of Egypt* (12).

The Lord set his heart on us in love. In return, we should stop being stubborn. We should know in our own hearts the sign of devotion and passionate commitment of a changed attitude from selfishness to selflessness; thinking less about ourselves and instead thinking more about others. A deeper experience and acknowledgement of God's grace in our own lives will lead us to be more caring about the lives of others. Grace makes us more concerned with ensuring justice. Faith produces good works. And let our people learn to devote themselves to good works, so as to help cases of urgent need, and not be unfruitful (13).

When Paul wrote to the Philippians, in Macedonia, he was thankful for their partnership in the gospel (14) with him, and what fruit that partnership bore. Paul's devotion to spreading the good news of the gospel was facilitated and even reliant on their other partnership with Paul in giving and receiving (15).

Paul was not interested in the gift of itself, but what it allowed him to do, what it told him of their care for him and what profit it accrued to the Philippians' account. What a beautiful mutually beneficial relationship, supporting each other for us to emulate today.

What grace from God, that with their devoted giving to him, a fragrant offering, a sacrifice acceptable and pleasing to God, Paul was able to say: *And my God will supply every need of yours according to his riches in glory in Christ Jesus. To our God and Father be glory for ever and ever. Amen* (16). One final challenge and encouragement to us from Paul which guides our priority in giving: *And let us not grow weary of doing good, for in due season we will reap, if we do not give up. So then, as we have opportunity, let us do good to everyone, and especially to those who are of the household of faith (17).*

References: (1) 2 Cor.8:6 (2) 2 Cor.8:1-2 NIV (3) 2 Cor.8:3-4 (4) 2 Cor.8:1 (5) 2 Cor.8:9 (6) Jn 1:16 (7) Acts 2:44-47 (8) 2 Cor.9:7 (9) Acts 4:32-35 (10) Waltke, B., Righteousness in Proverbs, Westminster Theological Journal 2008 (11) Jas.2:14-17 (12) Deut.10:16-19 (13) Tit.3:14 (14) Phil.1:5 (15) Phil.4:15 (16) Phil.4:18-20 (17) Gal.6:9-10

Bible quotations from the ESV, unless stated otherwise.

5.3 GIVING TO BUILD GOD'S HOUSE (ANDY SEDDON)

Throughout the history of God's relationship with His collective people is the evidence that He desires to dwell in the midst of them. Moses emphasized the privilege that had been given to the Israelites when he asked them rhetorically: *What great nation is there that has a god so near to it as the LORD our God is to us?* (1). Remarkably, God, who created this indescribably vast universe out of nothing, has chosen to create His earthly dwelling place out of the contributions which His people bring. Israel's response varied, and there are lessons to learn from their ups and downs.

When the People Gave

Exodus 35 and 1 Chronicles 29 contain uplifting narratives in which the nation of Israel give freely and generously for the building of the tabernacle and temple respectively. We consider both narratives hand in hand. The giving here was not compelled upon the people. They were freewill offerings. Concerning the building of the tabernacle in the wilderness, God commanded Moses from Mount Sinai to speak to Israel: *... that they take for me a contribution. From every man whose heart moves him you shall receive the contribution for me* (2). Moses passed on the appeal: *Whoever is of a generous heart, let him bring the Lord's contribution* (3). Years later, King David made a similar appeal in respect of the temple building work: *Who then will offer willingly, consecrating himself today to the Lord?* (4). The people responded beautifully in those days.

Exodus 35 states: *And they came, everyone whose heart stirred him, and everyone whose spirit moved him, and brought the Lord's contribution to be used for the tent of meeting* (5). Similarly in David's day the people rose to their leader's appeal; *for with a whole heart they had offered freely to the Lord* (6). What motivated the people to give so generously? It was their appreciation of God and therefore of God's house. King David, the man after God's "own heart" (7) gave lavishly from his own possessions to the building work of the temple, and he did it because of his *devotion to the house of my God* (8). It was his 'one thing' (9).

What am I truly devoted to? This question is searching and important, because it will dictate what I give to. Do I give reluctantly, or under some sort of obligation? Or do I relish the enormous privilege to give to something that God Himself takes so much pleasure in? David remembered that everything he gave was in fact God's to begin with (10). So it is with us today.

In Exodus 35:5-9 we have an inventory of materials God had selected which were the everyday items one would expect to see in the Israelite community, of varying degrees of value – for example, gold and silver from their jewellery, animal skins, oil and acacia wood. Everybody was able to bring something, regardless of their financial circumstances, from this inventory. Items that would have otherwise been used to enhance or beautify the lives and households of the family would be taken and made into something so much more glorious to beautify God's house and glorify Him.

No matter how insignificant we sometimes think our offering or contribution is, remember that God will take it, use it and transform its purpose into something for His own glory and pleasure. God does not expect more than we are able to give. We read in regard to the tabernacle that the material they had was sufficient to do all the work, and more (11). The people in the end had to be told to stop, as there was so much surplus! Therefore, we need not think that our offering to God's house is insufficient for the Lord's purposes.

Throughout the Scriptures joy is closely associated with giving and it was so in the day of the temple offerings. 1 Chronicles 29:9 records how the people rejoiced because they had given willingly, for with a whole heart they had offered freely to the Lord. David the King also rejoiced greatly. Nothing has changed – our own joy in God and in his House will follow our own gifts of devotion.

When the People Did Not Give

On a more sobering note, we come to the time of the returning exiles from Babylon who had begun rebuilding the temple in 538BC, but due to opposition they had given up this work. Twenty-two years later it required strong words from the Lord through Haggai to motivate them again; how had the mindset changed? The people were procrastinating. They were saying *the time has not yet come to rebuild the house of the Lord* (12). Do I sometimes delay what I might otherwise offer to God because I am waiting for a change in my circumstances or income? Let us not procrastinate, but prayerfully offer what we can without delay. The people were comfortable. They dwelt in their panelled houses (13) whilst God's house lay in ruins. There is nothing wrong with being comfortable, and living in nice houses if that is what we happen to have in life. However, comfort can turn into an idol which will dampen our passion for the house of God. When this happens there needs to be repentance and a revolution of our priorities. Jesus Himself commands us to *seek first the kingdom of God and his righteousness* (14).

Ironically, despite their apparent comfort, the people seemed to be ultimately dissatisfied and frustrated. Whilst the people focused on themselves, God remained passionate about His neglected house, so He withheld the blessings of the land, so that the people were forced to reconsider their position. *You have sown much, and harvested little. You eat, but you never have enough; you drink, but you never have your fill. You clothe yourselves, but no one is warm* (15). Striving for worldly happiness and contentment without prioritising God's things will always be a futile ambition. The returned exiles also seemed weak and discouraged. There were some among them who were old enough to remember the previous temple, which was more splendid to look at than the one they were rebuilding. God asks them *How do you see it now? Is it not as nothing in your eyes?* (16).

Does God's house seem small and numerically weak from where you are looking at it? Let us not be discouraged because the Lord takes great pleasure in His house, and He has promised to be with us when we get to work.

God's Spiritual House

Today, God continues to take pleasure in His house, and calls for generous givers to contribute to its building and maintenance. Of course, we are no longer talking about a material building. The apostle Peter shows us that the house today consists of people: *You yourselves like living stones are being built up as a spiritual house* (17). So then, what do we bring? We bring ourselves! Our bodies, our gifts, our time, our resources – financial and otherwise. Paul's appeal to the Romans is fitting here: *By the mercies of God ... present your bodies as a living sacrifice* (18).

Building God's house today centres around the growth of the people who make up the living stones. Outreach initiatives seek to find new stones to add to the building, and in-reach seeks to strengthen the existing structure through teaching, encouraging, supporting and shepherding. All of these activities require the generous giving of God's people to support them. The need is great, but the Exodus narratives suggest to us that all of the resources required are within the community, waiting to be generously supplied. David wrote: *O Lord, I love the habitation of your house and the place where your glory dwells* (19).

Do I have this love? Do I share the pleasure that God takes in His house? Does the beauty of His dwelling place today captivate me? May God stir my heart and move my spirit to give everything I can for His glory! Haggai's challenging words contained a promise to those who responded to the call to get building: *From this day on I will bless you* (20).

References: (1) Deut.4:7 (2) Ex.25:2 (3) Ex.35:5 (4) 1 Chron.29:5 (5) Ex.35:21 (6) Ex.29:9 (7) 1 Sam.13:14 (8) 1 Chron.29:3 (9) Ps.27:4 (10) 1 Chron.29:14 (11) Ex.36:7 (12) Hag.1:2 (13) Hag.1:4 (14) Matt.6:33 (15) Hag.1:6 (16) Hag.2:3 (17) 1 Pet.2:5 (18) Rom.12:1 (19) Ps.26:8 (20) Hag.2:19

Bible quotations from the ESV.

5.4 CHEERFUL GIVING (LENNIE SHAW)

Each one must give as he has decided in his heart, not reluctantly or under compulsion, for God loves a cheerful giver (1). The word translated 'cheerful' is the Greek hilaros, and means pretty much the same – cheerful, joyous. But it also has a sense of readiness. It means to be ready to act at a moment's notice, to be prepared.

> *Beware of practicing your righteousness before men to be noticed by them; otherwise you have no reward with your Father who is in heaven. So when you give to the poor, do not sound a trumpet before you, as the hypocrites do in the synagogues and in the streets, so that they may be honoured by men. Truly I say to you, they have their reward in full. But when you give to the poor, do not let your left hand know what your right hand is doing, so that your giving will be in secret; and your Father who sees what is done in secret will reward you* (2).

How should I be giving when it comes to the Lord's things? One thing is for sure, the Lord said in Matthew 6 *when you give...* not *if you give...*, so we certainly should be giving. One preacher I listened to recently emphasised the point that giving to God on a Lord's Day morning starts not when we break the bread at the Lord's table, not when the first brother gets on his feet in thanksgiving thereafter, but rather when we go to the offering box on the way in! What is my attitude of heart before God as I prepare to come near to Him in the holy place? Do I come ready to give? Perhaps as I carefully consider my financial offering to Him it reflects the condition of my heart as I prepare to bring my spiritual offering thereafter. If I find it difficult to give a financial offering, if I'm reluctant, or if I see it as a chore or a hardship, is my attitude of heart right in the first place?

The people of Malachi's day certainly saw it as a chore. *"You also say, 'Oh, what a weariness!' And you sneer at it,"* days the LORD of hosts. *"And you bring the stolen, the lame, and the sick; Thus you bring an offering! Should I accept this from your hand?" says the LORD"* (3). We shudder at the lazy, selfish attitude of the people in Malachi's day. "Oh, what a weariness!" they said, that they should have to give to the Lord of Hosts – and so they brought whatever they didn't really want themselves, thinking that would be good enough for Him. A token gesture if ever there was one. Is that how *the LORD, the God of all flesh* (4) deserves to be treated? Is that how He treated us when *He ... did not spare His own Son, but delivered Him up for us all*? (5).

The Lord encourages us to be 'cheerful givers', and I suppose if we really took the time to consider whom we ultimately give to, then it would gladden our hearts to the extent that we'd commit to extend our giving to Him still further. We can give to Him by giving to those we see who are in need:

> *"for I was hungry and you gave Me food; I was thirsty and you gave Me drink; I was a stranger and you took Me in; I was naked and you clothed Me; I was sick and you visited Me; I was in prison and you came to Me. Then the righteous will answer Him, saying, 'Lord, when did we see You hungry and feed You, or thirsty and give You drink? When did we see You a stranger and take You in, or naked and clothe You? Or when did we see You sick, or in prison, and come to You?' And the King will answer and say to them, 'Assuredly, I say to you, inasmuch as you did it to one of the least of these My brethren, you did it to Me'"* (6).

Faith without works is dead, the book of James illustrates on several occasions (7). Here is an opportunity to demonstrate both faith and works, by the denying of ourselves and instead being ready to give of what we have to Him through providing for others. Consider what Paul says about the churches in Macedonia, surely the blueprint for 'cheerful givers':

> *Moreover, brethren, we make known to you the grace of God bestowed on the churches of Macedonia: that in a great trial of affliction the abundance of their joy and their deep poverty abounded in the riches of their liberality. For I bear witness that according to their ability, yes, and beyond their ability, they were freely willing, imploring us with much urgency that we would receive the gift and the fellowship of the ministering to the saints. And not only as we had hoped, but they first gave themselves to the Lord, and then to us by the will of God* (8).

Despite the great trial of affliction there was an abundance of their joy in their willingness to go beyond that which they were able to give. Going beyond that of which we are naturally able is a God-given ability. People often talk of giving 110% to a task or a sport, but that's just motivational hyperbole. Going beyond our ability in God's things is very real, however. Of ourselves we are constrained by our human failings and weaknesses, but to go beyond our ability in the service of the Lord, in whatever area He calls us to be engaged, is something that is entirely reachable by the help of the Spirit that indwells us.

I don't think there's any coincidence that Paul says that they first gave themselves to the Lord, and then to us. The cheerful giver has already given himself/herself to the Lord, that's why they can rejoice in their giving, because all that we have is His, given to us by His gracious hand, and so we rejoice to give back to Him of what He has provided. These people didn't consider what they had, in terms of material possessions, or finances, to be particularly important at all, but rather they found their joy in the service of their God. Some nowadays might say they were naive, but in a world that is mired in unhappiness, hatred, selfishness and sin, give me their kind of joy every time! The condition of readiness is surely crucial.

If I'm too attached to my money – or my time for that matter – if I give material possessions a higher place than they should have, then I won't be ready to act at a moment's notice to give them to the Lord. *Give to everyone who asks of you. And from him who takes away your goods do not ask them back* (9). Again, many may be horrified at the thought of giving to someone who asks, and not seeing anything in return. It goes against everything our selfish culture teaches us, but that was the experience of the Lord on so many occasions. Whether it was healing those who were brought to Him, or teaching the multitudes for hours on end until He was exhausted, His life was all about giving to those who asked of Him, until He finally gave everything at Calvary.

What did the Lord say to the rich young ruler in Luke 18? *So when Jesus heard these things, He said to him, "You still lack one thing. Sell all that you have and distribute to the poor, and you will have treasure in heaven; and come, follow Me." But when he heard this, he became very sorrowful, for he was very rich* (10). Does the Lord ask us each to sell all that we have too? No, I don't believe so, but I do believe that He was highlighting this man's priorities. He wasn't just rich, he was very rich. Money was clearly his god, and the Lord, as He often did, put His finger right on the problem. The promise of future treasure in heaven wasn't enough to comfort this rich man, he was all about the riches of today and so, tragically, he went away sorrowful.

The NIV puts it: *he went away sad, because he had ...* (11). This stands in contrast to the cheerful giver who is already inclined to give to God and to others. Perhaps it's helpful for us, in considering how we can each be a cheerful giver, to remember just what we owe. To quote Romans 8:32 again: *He who did not spare his own Son but gave him up for us all, how will He not also with Him graciously give us all things?* The 'all things' here refers to peace, joy and purpose in this life, and salvation for eternity. A monetary donation, or even the giving of our precious time to someone who needs us, is nothing compared to all we receive because of Jesus' sacrifice.

References: (1) 2 Cor.9:7, ESV (2) Matt.6:1-4, NASB (3) Mal.1:13 (4) Jer.32:27 (5) Rom.8:32, ESV (6) Matt.25:35-40 (7) Jas.2:18-26 (8) 2 Cor.8:1-5 (9) Lk.6:30 (10) Lk.18:22-23 (11) Matt.19:22, NIV

Bible quotations from NKJV, unless otherwise stated.

PART 6: ABUNDANT MARRIAGES

Marriage was designed by God, not only to illustrate the relationship between Christ and His church, but also to help us navigate the ups and downs of life in a lifelong relationship that is centred on Him. God wants abundant marriages that don't only bear children, but bear fruit for Him. However, there are many statistics that illustrate just how elusive this is, given the amount of marriages (even Christian marriages) that end in separation or divorce, and these statistics do not and cannot capture the marriages that do continue, but are dry, loveless and bereft of the abundance and enjoyment that God intends.

The four chapters in this sixth segment cannot of course hope to solve every problem in every marriage; nevertheless, the sound Bible-based advice given in each of them is designed to point in the right direction.

Geoff Hydon explains in the first chapter just how important communication is to every marriage. Keith Dorricott outlines in chapter two how the twin aspects of unconditional love and unconditional respect need to work in tandem. In chapter 3, Dave Webster highlights how valuable both encouragement and forgiveness are in problem-solving in marriages, and Greg Neely completes this series by adding unselfishness and loyalty to the list of must-have attributes.

6.1 MAKING A MARRIAGE WORK – COMMUNICATION (GEOFF HYDON)

When Paul was writing about Satan's attacks on Christians he confidently stated: *we are not ignorant of his schemes*. He was right. Marriage was invented by God, so we know Satan will attack it. He encourages doubt about the need for marriage at all, and promotes immorality instead. Thus, he schemes to put us off marrying, or to make marriage a battleground instead of the divinely intended source of companionship. However, this series is about making marriages work, and how to avoid pitfalls. Our first topic is communication with one's spouse.

A 2006 study stated that on average women use over 20,000 words a day while men use only about 7,000. So picture the husband who has already used 6,995 words during his work day coming home with only about five words left, which might well be: "What's for dinner?" and "Good Night." Now please don't start arguing with your spouse about the likely inaccuracy of these statistics, or how often the illustration has proved true! You will just be confirming that people do communicate in different ways (not necessarily related to gender at all!). It's essential in marriage that we learn how our partner expects us to convey information, both about facts and feelings. If we develop this vital understanding it can contribute greatly to an overall positive relationship. If we ignore our spouse's expectations about communication frequency and methods we are in for testing times, and the Adversary has an advantage.

The biblical expectation of marriage is that a couple become 'one flesh.' This description could be the subject of a book by itself, but in this brief chapter we assume that a married couple should unselfishly live to produce mutual satisfaction. This needs communication reflecting shared goals and values. Paul cautioned widows in churches of God to marry 'only in the Lord', and surely this marriage principle applies more broadly than to widows. It should perhaps be obvious that communication will be under greater challenge if a couple does not share Biblically-based beliefs and values. Practising good communication should feature during an effective, prayerful courtship, where Christ reigns in all decision-making. It is never too early to recognize inherent or developing problems and begin tackling them.

How can we defend our marriages against communication breakdowns? Here we can only pick on a few potential weak spots. Obviously, it is important to be a good listener. Do we wait for our partner to finish speaking? Do we avoid assumptions and seek clarification, or leap to conclusions? Do we first share areas of agreement, before we explore why we disagree? Are conversations honest, and without secrets? If we feel we cannot talk about something with our spouse, that might indicate feelings of harmful independence rather than needed interdependence. Are important matters discussed in the right environment, not in hurried or heated exchanges at the wrong time or place to have any hope of resolving anything? Do we avoid inconsistency between what we do and what we say, or the way we say it?

Body language, tone of voice, evidence of emotions, all lead to reinterpretation of what is actually said. What if one spouse is more subjective and emotional while the other is more objective and analytical? Our upbringing or personality may create differences like these. We must learn how our spouse actually communicates, and not rely on simply what is said! So communication skills cannot be de-linked from exercise of patience, to ensure the other person has opportunity to get their meaning across. Arguments about whether husband or wife actually said specific words are usually ineffective, as the real failure is not in memory but in understanding what was meant. Good marriages need good apologies; we will all likely fail in the way we say things.

Marriage is perhaps the best forum for perfecting communication, because love can prevail. May you be blessed with encouragement, in seeing the Lord's provision of a loving marriage partner and in working at ensuring mutual delight in your companionship.

The writer has been happily married for over 40 years; the sequel to a teenage romance! The article has outlined practical wisdom, learned from mistakes and triumphs over the years, which is consistent with published empirical studies.

The following Scriptures support key statements: 2 Cor.2:11, NASB; Matt.19:4-6; 1 Cor.6:9-11; 7:39; Matt.15:19; Prov.3:6; 31:11; Amos 3:3; Jas.1:19,20; 3:8; 1 Pet.3:7; 4:8,9; Song of Songs 8:7

6.2 MAKING A MARRIAGE WORK – UNCONDITIONAL LOVE AND RESPECT (KEITH DORRICOTT)

Is it possible for two people who are equal in God's eyes to live together harmoniously, when one is acknowledged as the 'head' and the other as 'subject'? (1) It sounds very outdated, particularly in the Western world. And yet it is still God's way – and the way that marriage works; because marriage is far more than a man and a woman merely living parallel lives, just coming together on things they have in common, such as their children. God designed marriage for couples to enjoy oneness – personally, spiritually and physically.

And so through Peter He first tells wives to respect their own husbands (2). They do this by willingly submitting to their husbands' decisions and by treating them in a respectful way – unconditionally (even if they are disobedient to the Word). This does not mean the wife has to be passive or silent. The text in Peter may imply the wife's first responsibility is to use the Word of God verbally to win the husband's obedience to it, failing which she is to seek to win him by an example of fearless personal obedience to the Word, but without insubjection to her husband.

One of the ways that women can teach younger women is in how to properly show love to their husbands (3). And when a man feels that he has his wife's respect, he will find it easier to reciprocate by expressing his love to her. Feeling that respect is important to most husbands. A spirit of subjection is not limited to wives, of course. It is to be characteristic of us all as followers of Christ. Paul introduces the subject of submission by wives to their husbands by saying to all of us: *Be subject to one another in the fear of Christ* (1). And then God tells husbands that they are to love their wives, in the same way that they love themselves and also in the way that Christ loves His church. Christ gave His life for them, and husbands are to do the same for their wives, not by dying for them, but by living for them. They are not to act independently or selfishly. In his headship, a man is accountable to the Lord for the relationship, and it is a big responsibility to take on.

A husband's love for his wife is to be given unconditionally – no matter what. As he lives with his wife in an understanding way (2), he will get to know her more and more, and find out the ways in which she most feels loved. It may be in how he talks to her, or the time and attention he gives her, or the help he provides for her, how he meets her financial needs and helps her to feel safe, or it may be by physical contact, and it should include spiritual leadership.

But, with the best of intentions, this love will never be all that God has designed unless it is sourced by God Himself – unless it is God's love at work through him. As a husband demonstrates his love for God or experiences God's love for him, he is more consistently able to show his love for his wife. And failing to love her has consequences, he is told. God may refrain from answering his prayers because he is treating carelessly God's own daughter.

Christ Himself is the great example of both subjection and love. We see His attitude exemplified at Gethsemane when He poured out His passionate prayer that the cup would pass from Him. He did not suppress those feelings, and yet He submitted Himself to His Father's will. Similarly we see His sacrificial love in taking our place before His accusers (not leaving us to fend for ourselves). Thus husbands are to love their wives the way Christ did, and wives are to submit to their husbands as He did, *as to the Lord* (1).

Subjection and love must be from the heart, but also must be an act of will. And when they are, marriage can be enjoyed fully as God designed it – the husband and wife enjoying together the grace of life (2). It may not be the popular way nowadays, but it is still the way that works. It is God's way.

References: (1) Eph.5:21-33 (2) 1 Pet.3:1-7 (3) Titus 2:4

Bible quotations from the NASB.

6.3 MAKING A MARRIAGE WORK – ENCOURAGEMENT AND FORGIVENESS (DAVE WEBSTER)

"My wife can't cook." "My husband is useless around the house!" "You never listen to a word I say!" Harsh words, criticism and telling it as it is, even if dressed up as honesty or straight talking, are words that tend to pull down rather than build up, aren't they? It is not a great idea to 'put down' your spouse or to insist on having the last word or to stress the things that he or she is not good at. The Bible tells us that *the husband is the head of the wife as Christ is the head of the church, his body, of which he is the Saviour* (1). And this thought is developed in the following verses. Stop and reflect on that for a moment! Love her, care for her, look after her interests in the way that the Lord Jesus looks after the interests of the church! That rules out those harsh words (2), an uncaring attitude (3) or a discouraging put-down as both husbands and wives are commanded to respect each other.(4)

In our world of corporate 'Have Your Say' schemes people are more likely to make a complaint than to issue a compliment. We are more likely to make a fuss when we are treated discourteously than we are to return to say thanks for a good job well done! But it does not have to be like that in a Christian marriage. Sometimes all that is needed is the assurance of encouragement. "That was good," or "I'm glad you thought of that," doesn't cost anything, but can mean so much. And when it comes to our service for the Lord, husbands and wives can play a key role in encouraging each other not to give up or choose the wrong options. We can pray together, for each other, for our families and friends and our church and that really focuses us on what is important.

But what about those times when things go wrong? *Bear with each other and forgive whatever grievances you may have against one another. Forgive as the Lord forgave you* (5) is the general principle. A simple "sorry" is often all that is required between a couple who love and care for each other. If the hurt is deeper it may mean talking through the situation to explain why you feel let down, but above all the Lord's instruction is *Do not let the sun go down while you are still angry, and do not give the devil a foothold* (6). That means sorting out what has come between you and starting each day without yesterday's anger smouldering away – even if it means eating humble pie!

Practising what these two Scriptures teach:

(1) We overlook the little things and let them go as unimportant, both of us 'bearing with' and forgiving all the time.

(2) When we do have to consciously forgive, we remember how much God has forgiven us and suddenly the 'grievance' loses some of its sting. A forgiven couple must always be forgiving to each other!

(3) We never carry over hurts to fight again the next day – that is the way to spoil a marriage and invites disaster into our relationship.

(4) We remain alert that the Adversary is seeking to undermine our marriage and we do not let him get anything to latch on to.

Holding grudges and finding fault may be human traits, but forgiving and encouraging is God's way. Marriage is God's idea and it always works better when, together, we operate it God's way.

References: (1) Eph.5:23 (2) see Col.3:19 (3) See 1 Cor.7:33 (4) see 1 Pet. 3:7 & Eph.5:33 (5) Col.3:13 (6) Eph.4:26-27

Bible quotations from the NIV.

6.4 MAKING A MARRIAGE WORK – UNSELFISHNESS AND LOYALTY (GREG NEELY)

Solomon gave excellent counsel when he said: *By wisdom a house is built, and by understanding it is established; and by knowledge the rooms are filled with all precious and pleasant riches* (1). Good advice for a marriage too! And integral to putting these into practice are the imperatives of unselfishness and loyalty to one another and to the Lord. Marriage is after all a three-way union and the Lord's foundational place in it is ignored or minimized to our detriment.

The Lord's unselfishness, as our example, is memorably described by Paul. Christ is one who is equal with God, but who did not cling to or grasp that position. Instead *He ... emptied Himself, taking the form of a bond-servant, and ... humbled Himself* (2). There is no better definition of an unselfish mindset, nor example of unselfish behaviour. We do well to imitate it: not thinking of ourselves first, but thinking of our spouse; not merely looking out for our own personal interests, but also for the interests of our life partner (3). Of course, this is to be true of all our relationships; how much more vital in the one that is to be closest of all earthly ones! Be willing to be humble.

Paul was not married, but he certainly had the principles figured out! And the best principles in this case are actually the best practices! To the Corinthians he wrote: *but one who is married is concerned about the things of the world, how he may please his wife ... how she may please her husband* (4). This is as it ought to be in a marriage where unselfishness is a characteristic. Of course, we all need to have as our ambition, our aim, to please the Lord (5), whether married or not. But part of that responsibility in a marriage is pleasing our spouse, not merely ourselves, as we serve together. Do you know what really pleases your spouse? Is it flowers, just because; or is it putting the toothpaste cap on the countertop so there is no ring of paste left? Is it cleaning the whiskers out of the sink after you shave?! So often in relationships, as in life, it can be the smallest of kindnesses that makes the most impact.

Not only so, but our loyalty to our marriage partner must be unwavering and absolute. The cleaving of the man to his wife and the two becoming one flesh is how the divine designer put this relationship together (6). To 'cleave' (KJV) is to be 'glued together'. It is to be indissoluble: it is not to be chipped away at or cracked by a lack of commitment by either husband or wife. That's why the wife is to be subject to her husband and to respect him (7). That takes loyalty (and humility) for the woman, particularly when her husband does not deserve it. That's why the husband is to love his own wife as his own body (v.28), nourishing and cherishing her. The words in Greek can read 'love their own wives as being their own body'. That's what being loyal involves: treating your own wife as your own body. And again, the Lord Jesus is our supreme example – we are members of His body and He nourishes us and cherishes us, just as He also is submissive to God, being entirely equal!

When your spouse walks into a crowded room, do you sense that the room just got brighter and warmer? Are you kind and supportive in your speech and your actions? Do others wish they had a relationship like you have? Are you a good example, a role model, someone to imitate?

Wisdom will build or restore a relationship. Understanding one another will establish it, will set it in order. Knowing each other intimately will fill to overflowing the relationship with precious and pleasant riches. This honours the Lord who is to be entwined in the very fabric of Christian marriage. And as we submit to each other and selflessly and loyally complement our spouses, we are an example to the world of the unselfishness and loyalty of Jesus Christ to us!

References: (1) Prov.24:3-4 (2) Phil.2:7-8 (3) Phil.2:4 (4) 1 Cor.7:33-34 (5) 2 Cor.5:9 (6) Matt.19:5 (7) Eph.5:22,33

Bible quotations from the NASB.

PART 7 – ABUNDANT PERSONAL EVANGELISM

Our final and seventh segment explores the subject of personal evangelism, or witnessing. Although God endows some people with the specific gift of evangelism, this doesn't mean that he doesn't expect every Christian to engage regularly in some form of personal witnessing.

However, our series acknowledges the fact that personal witnessing can be a difficult thing to do; perhaps this is because of a fear of a rejection or not knowing how to broach and approach the topic in conversation. We might feel that the ground on which we are "sowing our seed" is hard, dry and barren, but we long for their to be fruit for our labours for the Lord. How can we partner with the work of the Holy Spirit in people's lives for this to be achieved?

In chapter one, Brian Johnston provides an overview of three main challenges that need to be overcome for someone to be persuaded of the gospel message and become a Christian. Tony Jones explores the first of these, the emotional objections to the gospel in chapter 2 that are often raised by people we already know, and people we may meet.

In chapter three, Karl Smith looks at the intellectual objections to the Christian faith and the employment of apologetics and personal testimony to combat them. Finally, Dave Webster examines the so-called volitional barriers to faith, which requires the will of the individual to be broken down and sets out the three steps needed – believe, repent, respond.

May God use this material to help in bringing many people to the Saviour!

7.1 OVERCOMING DEFENCES TO THE GOSPEL (BRIAN JOHNSTON)

The success of the Gospel in capturing a person's heart has been likened to the process of capturing a castle (1). Access to a castle in historic times was gained only as each barrier that formed its physical defences was overcome. As with all analogies, there are doubtless limitations. Each defence may not be tackled independently of the others or indeed in the order we shall take them in this and subsequent articles. However, we trust this analogy is sufficiently helpful in understanding the process of bringing the Gospel to non-Christians that it will repay us to think in these terms.

The First Line of Defence - Bridging the Emotional Moat

The first barrier, which we may liken to a moat, is the emotional defence. The person to whom we are witnessing may be hurting. For example, a person's relationship with his or her father may, sadly, have been such that the presentation of God as the heavenly Father of all who believe in Christ as Saviour arouses strong negative emotions, making it difficult for them to place trust in God.

This moat may be overcome by building a bridge of love that touches people's hearts. We need to accept people even when we can't approve of their behaviours. When we relate to others or meet people, we may not be sharing the gospel immediately but we should still be intentional in building a 'bridge' to get there at some later time. This is why we engage in some pre-evangelistic strategies such as community good works. The bridge we build has got to be strong enough to bear the weight of gospel truth, so we aim to befriend people. The greatest love we can express for our neighbour is to introduce them to Christ. Christ's love controls us, Paul said (2), and we are to be channels of that love to others.

The Second Line of Defence - Breaching the

Intellectual Wall

What we may compare with the castle wall is intellectual resistance to the Gospel. Where, in this scientifically enlightened age, is the evidence for God's existence? How can there be an all-loving and all-powerful God when there is so much evil, suffering and injustice in the world?

In order to gain access to the mind with truth, apologetics-type arguments have a place. Peter urged his readers to be able to give a reasoned basis for the Christian hope (3). Apologetics is not evangelism, but is often a necessary support for it. Our appeal, as Paul's, is to their conscience which we seek to enlist on the side of truth (4). The use of questions can expose the incoherence of all other worldviews. We can be bold, for the intellectual strength of Christianity is stronger than all other options, despite some dismissing it as foolishness (5).

The Final Line of Defence - Scaling the Volitional Tower

Like an imposing tower, the volitional defence presents itself. This is the barrier of the will. Our work of showing care and communicating authentically has been done; any further work must now be God's. Our part now is urgent, passionate prayer as we invite someone to come to Christ (6). We are asking them to do something which they, by themselves, are incapable of doing. God is sovereign, but holds us responsible. No more than 'God wills' to be saved will be saved; but equally, no less than 'whoever wills' will be saved.

It's at this stage that providing illustrations of the gospel often proves helpful. The volitional barrier, the tower, is overcome as the will is surrendered and Christ's lordship is recognized (7). This is done whenever God grants repentance: a radical turning from sin to God (8). The call to repentance should never be diluted whenever we counsel sinners whom we believe are under conviction of sin (9). They must be left in no doubt as to their need (10) and inability (11); as well as God's provision (12) and requirement, namely to repent and believe on the Lord Jesus (7).

References: (1) D.A. Carson (Ed), Telling the Truth, Zondervan, 2002 (2) 2 Cor. 5:14 (3) 1 Pet.3:15 (4) 2 Cor.4:2 (5) 1 Cor.1:25 (6) Rom.10:1 (7) Acts 16:31 (8) 2 Tim. 2:25 (9) Acts 20:21; John 16:8 (10) Rom.3:23 (11) Isa.64:6 (12) Jn 3:16

Bible quotations from the NASB.

7.2 CROSSING THE EMOTIONAL MOAT (TONY JONES)

This sub-series of chapters makes the analogy of winning someone's heart for Christ with the methods used to enter a fortified castle. The first line of defence was the moat. This separated the walls of the castle from unfriendly forces and a bridge was necessary to cross it. For a welcome guest, the drawbridge would be lowered by those who were in the castle; whilst those who were on the offensive would try to fill in the moat or build their own bridge.

What Causes Emotional Defences?

In our analogy, the moat that surrounds a person is that individual's emotional defences. These defences are ways to keep people at arm's length until trust replaces initial doubts and suspicions. The moat will consist of personal experiences that have shaped someone's outlook and his willingness to build friendships with new contacts. In our world, many have experienced significant hurt caused by others as the selfish character of the last days grows (1). Deeper relationships are so easily cast aside today. So many parents neglect their responsibilities to their children, some of whose lives are terminated before they even get their first breath; divorce courts register increasingly the headlong race to annul vows that seemingly were not taken for lifelong fulfilment, and who knows how many broken hearts are created as people flit in and out of temporarily convenient 'living together' arrangements? What, but the love of God, can truly heal these terrible scars? Who is there to show it, if not us?

How Do we Cross the Moat?

However, the analogy of us crossing someone's moat could be misleading. A drawbridge is not lowered when the enemy is advancing aggressively. As Christians, though, given Christ's love for the unsaved, we need to be ready to establish long-term relationships. This has to be based on a trust as close as possible to the absolute trust that they would be able to have in the Lord if He were physically alongside. We need to start to build a bridge, a strong bridge based on the Spirit's fruit (2) which gives the person confidence in our character and motive. 'Success' would be evident when they let down their drawbridge to close the remaining gap and metaphorically welcome us. We will be presented with numerous occasions to exhibit wisdom requested from God in the quest to reach those we know for Him (3) and we have to be faithful in our witness (4).

We may not even become aware of a person's salvation in this life. God has His plans and uses us as He wills. We need to fulfil obediently the role He has for us by building those connections, using our experiences too (5). Bill Hybels says: 'I believe many people begin their spiritual quest at a negative ten and that it is my role to facilitate their movement to a negative eight. That's it. Two points on the spectrum, and a result that is still in negative territory' (6). Our part is to lay a foundation that can be built upon by the God who crowns work with His blessing (7); this includes challenges for us which, without God's Spirit, would be futile (8) – accurately representing the person of Christ to them, introducing them to the lover of their souls and loving them with His love. Of course, we will not be perfect ambassadors, so the assistance of the Spirit is crucial – awareness of weaknesses, confession of failure and a devotion not to let the Master down. One bad example of a disciple's behaviour could extinguish any desire by a seeker.

People

We are surrounded by the people God has determined to be there, for His purposes. These are our immediate contacts (9) so we don't have to go looking for people to reach out to. What is needed, though, is to thoughtfully consider whom we interact with, the types of relationships we have, and their needs that we know of. We can then bring all this to the Lord, asking Him to lead us to have a burden for specific people and look for developing relationships for His glory. That might not be the ones we think are most obvious, so don't rule people in or out based on personal feelings, though common interests will assist. There is a variety of groups with whom we spend time, which will differ depending on our stage in life, health, mobility, etc.

Neighbours

This is a tougher arena to work in than it used to be. The trend today seems to be towards being more insulated from neighbours, not necessarily by choice, but perhaps as the result of the frenetic society we live in. The pressure of work in the Western world means that opportunities for a 'chat over the garden fence' are more limited. Many people choose to interact with others by electronic media while being entertained by the TV after a hard day's work. Generating communication with neighbours requires conscious effort, and those things which work against God, including our selfish self (10), would feed us all sorts of excuses to avoid that endeavour.

Making contact could take place soon after moving into a new property by distributing a brief, attractive letter/note about yourself/family including a reference to your relationship with the Lord and church membership. This could be followed by some invitations into your home for coffee or a meal. If new people move into the locality, make a brief visit with a small welcome gift and a word of introduction. There are often invitations to neighbourhood group events to respond to and with prayer, wise involvement can lead to widening opportunities to build bridges. The number of ways to reach out is large, but it is all too easy to generate plausible excuses not to do so – even things like, "I just have too much to do in church to do that as well."

Work Colleagues/Fellow Students

We must not forget the primary reason for being in these groups – to learn or to work. This is itself a great opportunity to build trust by being someone who is a model student/employee; doing the work efficiently without complaint, not slacking when the boss is not looking, etc. In the Bible, Joseph excelled in this and Paul exhorts us to continue to do so (11). An attitude of humility developed by the Spirit of God is essential, to prevent getting people's backs up (12). Pray for, and seek out, positive conversations which do not disturb duty. Socialising opportunities arise when bridges can be strengthened. The locations are often 'neutral/tending to unhelpful', which brings the risk of destroying work already done. Engaging in such events ought to take place only after specific prayer asking for the Holy Spirit's help to keep holy and focused on the task of crossing the moat with people, not indulging in self-satisfying pursuits (13).

Family and Friends

This can be a tough group to build the bridges that lead to evangelism as you will be best known here, warts and all. The advantage is that the drawbridge is perhaps more easily lowered. Twenty-first century communication is often electronic, so careful use of this is paramount. The written word loses intonation and so is easily misinterpreted; use of social media networks is tending to allow people to reveal issues that they might not talk about. This can be insightful, but it's all too easy for a Christian to undo good groundwork with unwise text. Poor venue choices to meet with friends could also easily undermine the foundations of any bridge.

Places

Before most people had cars, it was usual to live, work and go to church meetings and activities in the same locality; clearly an advantage in building bridges to people with the same groups involved in all three. We should consider this a higher priority in our prayers when making significant decisions. Today mobility is easy, so our work, our church's meeting location, and where we live, can be some (considerable) distances from each other. Circumstances may seem to dictate how these work out, but selfish factors are easily applied, yet not easily recognised, in decision-making. "How can I get a better property for the same money?" "How can I get a better job than those which are local to where the church meets?" etc.

Distant locations mean it's that much harder to invite work colleagues/neighbours with whom we are bridge-building to appropriate events taking place in the church's meeting place. We may not even consider asking people along as it is "just too far" to expect them to come. How much of an impact over the recent years has this had on our opportunity to move past building the bridge?

References (1) 2 Tim.3:2-5 (2) Gal.5:22-23; 2 Pet.1:5-7 (3) Jas.1:5; Prov.11:30 (4) 1 Cor.4:2 (5) 2 Cor.1:3-4 (6) Bill Hybels, Just Walk Across the Room, Zondervan, 2006 (7) 1 Cor.3:6 (8) Gal.3:3 (9) Acts 17:26 (10) Rom.7:18 (11) Gen.39:3-4,21-23; Col.3:22-23 (12) Phil.2:3 (13) Rom.15:1-3

7.3 SCALING THE INTELLECTUAL WALL (KARL SMITH)

Some people don't want to believe that the Christian faith is true. They think it will mean they can't do things they want to do. Consequently, they are satisfied with a handful of secular ideas picked up at school, on television or at the pub and dismiss the 'need' to believe in God as a historical hangover from more ignorant times. For others, however, genuine intellectual difficulties baffle any attempt to take the message of the Gospel seriously. Their intellectual honesty forbids them from believing a comforting lie and they feel that too many aspects of our belief contradict key foundations of their education. It is our responsibility to help them to overcome these objections so that they may be won for the Lord who loves them.

The apostle Peter stresses the importance of preparation in this, saying *be prepared to make a defense to anyone who asks you for a reason for the hope that is in you yet do it with gentleness and respect* (1). People will see how we cope with life and the hope that keeps us going. Nevertheless, in asking us about it, they will expect us to defend our trust in the Lord Jesus with a reason. In this scripture, how we are to do it is as important as what we are to do. How often has Christian witness been ineffective because we have forgotten to do it *with gentleness and respect*?

In 2010, evangelist Malcolm Macdonald and I conducted a door-to-door survey in Paisley, Scotland, asking people what their reasons were for not believing in God. This was to help us plan a series of seminars called 'Big Questions' at which the top eight answers would be dealt with by a talk and open discussion. Answers mainly fell into four categories:

a) **Philosophical**: e.g. "If there is a God, why is there so much suffering?" This was by far the most common answer and can only really be dealt with by sympathetic listening and sensitive discussion of the wounds of Christ.

b) **Scientific**: e.g. "Sciences such as geology and biology seem to tell a different story from that of Genesis." It is hard to expect people to believe the message of the Bible when page one seems to contradict everything they learned in school. It is particularly important here to be honest about gaps in our knowledge, but to focus on how the Bible answers the questions science doesn't attempt to answer; not so much how life emerged, as why? Besides, I personally feel that although scientists are basing their theories on the best evidence available, God has more information at His disposal and is more likely to be right, having been there when the universe emerged. Extrapolating backwards from contemporary processes to determine how such processes operated in the past is all very well, for example, but pre-supposes as part of its methodology that changes to the order of nature detailed in Genesis and elsewhere did not happen.

c) **Historical**: "Religion causes wars and violence." This is perhaps the easiest of these to counter since the secular and openly atheistic regimes of the twentieth century have been even worse.

d) **Textual:** "Isn't the Bible full of errors/manipulation?" Whilst most people who made this point were confusing the fictitious world of Dan Brown's 'The Da Vinci Code' with the real one, there are indeed a small number of variant readings between original manuscripts of which more thoughtful people may be aware. Nevertheless most editions of the Bible point these up and argue only for lapses in the copying rather than in the original act of inspiration. Comparison with the basis on which other documents from the same era are accepted as authentic shows how amazingly God has preserved His Word.

It is good to be aware of these ideas, most of which came to prominence in the Western world in the nineteenth century. We don't need to answer them point by point, but sometimes we will need to earn an audience by showing that we have engaged with these ideas and they have not shaken our belief. Paul in Corinth reasoned in the synagogue every Sabbath, and tried to persuade Jews and Greeks (2). There is a place for reasoning and persuasion in defence of the Gospel.

Recently Richard Dawkins and John Lennox, both Professors at Oxford University, debated the question 'Has science buried God?' Professor Dawkins began, naturally enough for a professor in biology, by making an apparently convincing case that natural selection alone is able to explain the emergence of the human race. It became clear, however, at the conclusion of Professor Dawkins' opening remarks that his real objection to Christianity was not to do with biology at all. Rather, it was our belief that a God who created this exceedingly complex, yet orderly, universe should be interested enough in human sin and suffering to become man and die for His creatures. It was the opportunity to answer this aspect of Professor Dawkins' speech with an explanation of Calvary that provided the most powerful part of Professor Lennox's argument. It reminded me of Paul's words in 1 Corinthians 1:18-24:

> *... the word of the cross is folly to those who are perishing, but to us who are being saved it is the power of God. ... Where is the debater of this age? ... For since, in the wisdom of God, the world did not know God through wisdom, it pleased God through the folly of what we preach to save those who believe. For Jews demand signs and Greeks seek wisdom, but we preach Christ crucified, a stumbling block to Jews and folly to Gentiles, but to those who are called, both Jews and Greeks, Christ the power of God and the wisdom of God.*

However well prepared we are in the field of apologetics (and we must be prepared), it is ultimately in the cross itself that the power of the Gospel resides. It does indeed defeat our finite rational minds to imagine that God cares about the intimate thoughts of specks of dust on a speck of dust – still more that He should dearly love us. Yet it is the message of the cross that rings true with an appeal to the spirit. Neither does it defy logic, as anyone who reads the book of Romans from beginning to end must acknowledge. It is, however, a divine logic which leaves the loveless logic of man standing at the starting line. In the Wisdom of God, the cross has satisfied God in all the characteristics that our finite minds might find contradictory: His holiness, His justice, His mercy and His love. We must keep steering the conversation back to this 'foolishness' because it is this upon which the Spirit of God works to bring conviction of sin, righteousness and judgement.

Our series began by thinking of intellectual barriers our listeners might have to the gospel as a wall that we need to scale. The image the Bible uses is a 'veil', a curtain covering over the truth, meaning that people 'just can't see it':

> *And even if our gospel is veiled, it is veiled to those who are perishing. In their case the god of this world has blinded the minds of the unbelievers, to keep them from seeing the light of the gospel of the glory of Christ, who is the image of God* (3).

Satan is using everything in his power to prevent people from seeing the glory of what Christ achieved on the cross and from recognising His heavenly splendour. Earlier Paul spoke compassionately of the veil over the minds of his own nation, the Jews: *But their minds were hardened. For to this day, when they read the old covenant, that same veil remains unlifted. As a result, a veil lies over their hearts* (4). Hardened minds leading to unresponsive hearts – could there be a more accurate description of the hard soil we are breaking up today? Thankfully, Paul also provides the answer to the problem: *only through Christ is it taken away* (4). By all means deal with the objections people have, but return often to the lovely personality of Christ, to the cross and Jesus glorified there.

Finally, don't lose confidence in the truth of the Gospel. My knowledge of science could be written on the back of a postage stamp and anyone who has achieved decent high school grades in any one of the sciences could make mincemeat of me in debate on the Genesis account of creation, for example. Indeed, this has happened many times! Nevertheless, our powers of reasoning are part of that finite, fallen human entity called 'the flesh'. We are equipped with something stronger:

> *For the weapons of our warfare are not of the flesh but have divine power to destroy strongholds. We destroy arguments and every lofty opinion raised against the knowledge of God, and take every thought captive to obey Christ* (5).

Whereas Peter focused on defence of our hope, Paul takes us on to the attack. This is the message of the cross, expressed in the Scriptures. Now more than ever we must take it out to a blinded world and shine its light into the minds of our friends, neighbours and fellow human beings across the world.

References: (1) 1 Pet.3:15 (2) Acts 18:4 (3) 2 Cor.4:3-4 (4) 2 Cor.3:14-15 (5) 2 Cor.10:4-5

Bible quotations from the ESV.

7.4 STORMING THE TOWER OF THE WILL (DAVE WEBSTER)

I'm good at hesitating! I can do all the research into the product I am interested in and I can convince myself that I know the right one to go for, but still I hesitate. I return to the shop or I go online again and find nothing has changed, but I'm still reluctant to press that button or commit to the purchase. I'm not sure. I am unwilling to proceed. I'll have another look later! Maybe I'll never get round to it.

In the analogy we have been using in this series we have thought about barriers to accepting the Gospel as being like defences to a castle. We saw how the emotional moat consists of personal experiences that have shaped someone's outlook and how that needs to be bridged by the love of God. Last time we considered how to scale the intellectual wall to get over objections that stop people coming to the Lord; things like the idea that science has disproved God, or that the Bible is unreliable. Now we have arrived at the strong tower we sometimes call 'volitional' – which simply means the tower of the will and the need to make a conscious choice or decision.

The trouble is we are not very good at doing this. The Bible gives us three reasons why this is the case:

- We are hesitant, we like to 'hedge our bets', we like to think about God and see what else is on offer; or, maybe, not think too much about God because we have other important things in life to concern ourselves with. But this will not do, we need to take action and we need to act decisively.

- We are rebellious! We don't live God's way or do the things God says we ought to do. We have put ourselves in the position of being enemies of almighty God and we need to repent.

- We are dead! Not physically dead, of course, but unable to respond to God, and totally incapable of saving ourselves. And we need to be made alive.

Believe and Act Decisively

We are living in an age of tolerance, except that there is little tolerance for anyone who says they have found the right way! But God's Word is clear that the Lord Jesus is ... *the way and the truth* ... (1) and that a definite decision has to be made by us on that basis. *Believe me* ... (2) said the Lord Jesus. *Believe in the Lord Jesus, and you will be saved* (3), was the message of the apostles. *We believe that Jesus died and rose again* (4), wrote the apostle Paul, and John's conclusion was that the Scripture account of the life of the Lord Jesus was *that you may believe that Jesus is the Messiah, the Son of God, and that by believing you may have life in his name* (5).

It takes a decisive act of the will to believe: not just anything we are told, of course, but what God has revealed to us in the Bible which is the Word of God. God expects us to investigate and make a decision on what he reasonably tells us. For example, the big crunch point of Christianity is the death and resurrection of Jesus Christ. Is this just something which we cannot really test, but just have to accept by blind faith against all the evidence? Not at all – by all the standards of objective investigation, this stands up as a historical fact which it is perfectly reasonable to believe (6). In addition, God's Word makes it a crunch fact for belief: *If you declare with your mouth, "Jesus is Lord," and believe in your heart that God raised him from the dead, you will be saved* (7).

Repent and Claim God's Forgiveness

No-one likes to be told they are wrong. In the moral and spiritual areas of life we are told nowadays that there is no right or wrong and each to his own! But that's not what God says to 21st century mankind in the Bible. Isaiah's summary, *All of us have become like one who is unclean* (8) is echoed by Paul to the Romans, *all have sinned and fall short of the glory of God* (9). That puts us in real trouble, facing God's anger for our sin. Except for the fact that God loves us, there would be no hope. But hope is held out in the command to repent. 'Repent' was the message of John the Baptist (10). 'Repent' was the keyword in Peter's sermon on the Day of Pentecost (11).

Paul's contribution to the meeting of the Areopagus in Athens was the same: talking about God, he said *now he commands all people everywhere to repent. For he has set a day when he will judge the world with justice by the man he has appointed. He has given proof of this to all men by raising him from the dead* (12). To repent is to be sorry, to turn away from the wrong thing and to start looking at reality God's way. In preaching the Gospel message we need to emphasise the importance of repentance without which forgiveness is not possible.

Respond and Become Alive Spiritually

As for you, you were dead in your transgressions and sins (13), wrote the Apostle to those who had repented and believed – dead in the sense of being unresponsive to God and totally incapable of helping themselves! Adam and Eve were warned not to eat from the tree of the knowledge of good and evil, *for when you eat of it you will certainly die* (14). And ever since that time, human beings have lived in this world in a state of spiritual death. *But because of his great love for us, God, who is rich in mercy, made us alive with Christ even when we were dead in transgressions – it is by grace you have been saved* (15).

That is the amazing response of our God. And we need to stress this, too: grace is the undeserved offer of salvation to each of us; accepting that offer is a decision of the will. The Lord Jesus asked this question one day: *I am the resurrection and the life. He who believes in me will live, even though he dies; and whoever lives and believes in me will never die. Do you believe this?* (16)

It's a good question to challenge someone who thinks living is just about here and now.

Storming That Tower of the Will

Believe, repent, respond. That's the issue. In telling the Gospel message we have to insist that the hearer gives up any ideas of doing it their own way. No matter how many times we hear it said, all roads do not lead to God; they need to find the right way. And it is volitional: an act of the will, a decision to be made, a response that is required. People need to turn in belief to the one who is 'the truth'; they need to repent of going their own way and 'doing their own thing' and they need to respond to the one who makes dead things live.

So why do we hesitate? If we don't take the time to listen, we can't believe; if we don't believe, we will never repent and if there is no repentance, we cannot become spiritually alive!

The apostle John saw the importance of looking at the evidence, making a choice, responding in repentance and receiving new life. He wrote in his Gospel that the Lord Jesus said *If anyone chooses to do God's will, he will find out whether my teaching comes from God or whether I speak on my own* (17).

That's an encouraging note to end on, isn't it? Although we cannot see God's things through our natural senses, people can choose to follow what God tells them and look into what God says and the promise is that they will have it revealed to them.

References: (1) Jn 14:6 (2) Jn 14:11 (3) Acts 16:31 (4) 1 Thess.4:14 (5) Jn 20:31, NIV 2011 (6) See, for example, The Case for Christ Lee Strobel, Zondervan (7) Rom.10:9 (8) Isa.64:6 (9) Rom.3:23 (10) See Matt.3:1-2 (11) Acts 2:38 (12) Acts 17:30-31 (13) Eph.2:1 (14) Gen.2:17 (15) Eph.2:4-5 (16) Jn 11:25-26 (17) Jn 7:17

Bible quotations are from the NIV.

Did you love *Abundant Christianity*? Then you should read *15 Hot Topics For Today's Christian*[1] by Hayes Press!

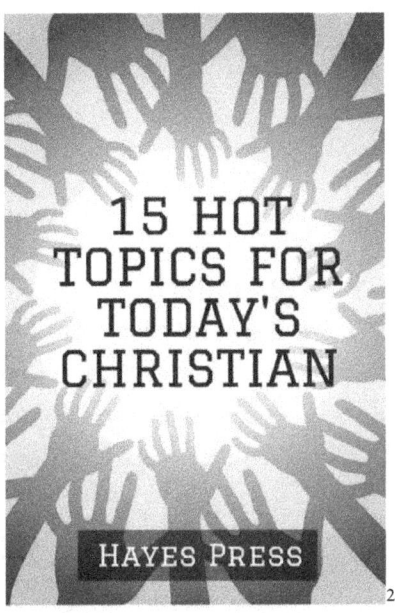

[2]

This book deals biblically with 15 practical and theological topics that most Christians will encounter in their discipleship experience, including: eternal security, the problem of suffering, the need for baptism, the prosperity gospel, the Trinity, divorce, voting, predestination and election, universalism, military service and more!

---

1. https://books2read.com/u/mgrOM6

2. https://books2read.com/u/mgrOM6

Also by Hayes Press

Bible Studies
Bible Studies 1990 - First Samuel
Bible Studies 1991 - The First Letter of Paul to the Corinthians
Bible Studies 1993 - Second Samuel
Bible Studies 1994 - The Establishment and Development of Churches of God
Bible Studies 1995 - The Kings of Judah and Israel from Solomon to Asa
Bible Studies 1992 - The Second Letter of Paul to the Corinthians

Needed Truth
Needed Truth 1888
Needed Truth 2001
Needed Truth 2002
Needed Truth 2003
Needed Truth 2004
Needed Truth 2005
Needed Truth 2006
Needed Truth 2007
Needed Truth 2008
Needed Truth 2009
Needed Truth 2010
Needed Truth 2011
Needed Truth 2012
Needed Truth 2015

Needed Truth 1888-1988: A Centenary Review of Major Themes

Standalone
The Road Through Calvary: 40 Devotional Readings
Lovers of God's House
Different Discipleship: Jesus' Sermon on the Mount
The House of God: Past, Present and Future
The Kingdom of God
Knowing God: His Names and Nature
Churches of God: Their Biblical Constitution and Functions
Four Books About Jesus
Collected Writings On ... Exploring Biblical Fellowship
Collected Writings On ... Exploring Biblical Hope
Collected Writings On ... The Cross of Christ
Builders for God
Collected Writings On ... Exploring Biblical Faithfulness
Collected Writings On ... Exploring Biblical Joy
Possessing the Land: Spiritual Lessons from Joshua
Collected Writings On ... Exploring Biblical Holiness
Collected Writings On ... Exploring Biblical Faith
Collected Writings On ... Exploring Biblical Love
These Three Remain...Exploring Biblical Faith, Hope and Love
The Teaching and Testimony of the Apostles
Pressure Points - Biblical Advice for 20 of Life's Biggest Challenges
More Than a Saviour: Exploring the Person and Work of Jesus
The Psalms: Volumes 1-4 Boxset
The Faith: Outlines of Scripture Doctrine
Key Doctrines of the Christian Gospel
Is There a Purpose to Life?
An Introduction to Bible Covenants
The Hidden Christ - Volume 2: Types and Shadows in Offerings and Sacrifices
The Hidden Christ Volume 1: Types and Shadows in the Old Testament
The Hidden Christ - Volume 3: Types and Shadows in Genesis
Heavenly Meanings - The Parables of Jesus

Fisherman to Follower: The Life and Teaching of Simon Peter
Called to Serve: Lessons from the Levites
Needed Truth 2017 Issue 1
The Breaking of the Bread: Its History, Its Observance, Its Meaning
Spiritual Revivals of the Bible
An Introduction to the Book of Hebrews
The Holy Spirit and the Believer
Exploring The Psalms: Volume 1 - Thoughts on Key Themes
Exploring The Psalms: Volume 2 - Exploring Key Elements
Exploring the Psalms: Volume 3 - Surveying Key Sections
The Psalms: Volume 4 - Savouring Choice Selections
Profiles of the Prophets
The Hidden Christ - Volumes 1-4 Box Set
The Hidden Christ - Volume 4: Types and Shadows in Israel's Tabernacle
Baptism - Its Meaning and Teaching
Conflict and Controversy in the Church of God in Corinth
In the Shadow of Calvary: A Bible Study of John 12-17
Moses: God's Deliverer
Sparkling Facets: Bible Names and Titles of Jesus
A Little Book About Being Christlike
Keys to Church Growth
From Shepherd Boy to Sovereign: The Life of David
Back to Basics: A Study of Core Bible Teaching and Practice
An Introduction to the Holy Spirit
Israel and the Church in Bible Prophecy
"Growth and Fruit" and Other Writings by John Drain
15 Hot Topics For Today's Christian
Needed Truth Volume 2 1889
Studies on the Return of Christ
Studies on the Resurrection of Christ
Needed Truth Volume 3 1890
The Nations of the Old Testament: Their Relationship with Israel and Bible Prophecy
The Message of the Minor Prophets
Insights from Isaiah

The Bible - Its Inspiration and Authority
Lessons from Ezra and Nehemiah
A Bible Study of God's Names For His People
Moses in One Hour
Abundant Christianity
Prayer in the New Testament

About the Publisher

Hayes Press (www.hayespress.org) is a registered charity in the United Kingdom, whose primary mission is to disseminate the Word of God, mainly through literature. It is one of the largest distributors of gospel tracts and leaflets in the United Kingdom, with over 100 titles and hundreds of thousands despatched annually. In addition to paperbacks and eBooks, Hayes Press also publishes Plus Eagles Wings, a fun and educational Bible magazine for children, and Golden Bells, a popular daily Bible reading calendar in wall or desk formats. Also available are over 100 Bibles in many different versions, shapes and sizes, Bible text posters and much more!

www.ingramcontent.com/pod-product-compliance
Lightning Source LLC
Chambersburg PA
CBHW031400040426
42444CB00005B/358